Principles of High-Performance Processor Design

Junichiro Makino

Principles of High-Performance Processor Design

For High Performance Computing, Deep Neural Networks and Data Science

 Springer

Junichiro Makino
Kobe University
Kobe, Hyogo, Japan

ISBN 978-3-030-76873-7   ISBN 978-3-030-76871-3   (eBook)
https://doi.org/10.1007/978-3-030-76871-3

This Springer imprint is published by the registered company Springer Nature Switzerland AG
The registered company address is: Gewerbestrasse 11, 6330 Cham, Switzerland

The future cannot be predicted, but futures can be invented. — Dennis Gabor

Preface

In this book, I tried to theorize what I have learned from my experience of developing special- and general-purpose processors for scientific computing. I started my research career as a graduate student in astrophysics, studying the dynamical evolution of globular clusters. The research tool was the N-body simulation, and it was (and still is) important to make simulations faster so that we can handle larger number of stars. I used vector supercomputers such as Hitac S-810, Fujitsu VP-400, NEC SX-2, Cray X-MP, Cyber 205, and ETA-10, and also tried parallel computers such as TMC CM-2 and PAX. Around the end of my Ph.D. course, my supervisor, Daiichiro Sugimoto, started the GRAPE project to develop special-purpose computers for astrophysical N-body simulations, and I was deeply involved in the development of numerical algorithms, hardware, and software. The GRAPE project is a great success, with hardware achieving 10–100 times better price- and watt-performance compared to general-purpose computers at the same time and used by many researchers. However, as semiconductor technology advanced into deep-submicron range, the initial cost of development of ASICs had become too high for special-purpose processors. In fact, it has become too high for most general-purpose processors, and that was clearly the reason why first the development of parallel computers with custom processors and then the development of almost all RISC processors were terminated. Only x86 processors from Intel and AMD had survived. (Right now, we might be seeing the shift from x86 to Arm, though) The x86 processors in the 2000s were not quite efficient in the use of transistors or electricity. Nowadays, we have processors with very different architectures such as GPGPUs and Google TPU, which are certainly more efficient compared to general-purpose x86 or Arm processors, at least for a limited range of applications. I also was involved in the development of a programmable SIMD processor, GRAPE-DR, in 2000s, and more recently a processor for deep learning, MN-Core, which was ranked #1 in the June 2020 and June 2021 Green500 lists.

In this book, I discuss how we can make efficient processors for high-performance computing. I realized that we did not have a widely accepted definition of the efficiency of a general-purpose computer architecture. Therefore, in the first three chapters of this book, I tried to give one possible definition, the ratio between the minimum possible energy consumption and the actual energy consumption for a given application using a given semiconductor technology. In Chapter 4, I overview general-purpose processors in the past and present from this viewpoint. In Chapter 5, I discuss how we can actually design processors with near-optimal efficiencies, and in Chapter 6 how we can program such processors. I hope this book will give a new perspective to the field of high-performance processor design.

This book is the outcome of collaborations with many people in many projects throughout my research career. The following is an incomplete list of collaborators: Daiichiro Sugimoto, Toshikazu Ebisuzaki, Yoshiharu Chikada, Tomoyoshi Ito, Sachiko Okumura, Shigeru Ida, Toshiyuki Fukushige, Yoko Funato, Hiroshi Daisaka, and many others (GRAPE, GRAPE-DR, and related activities); Piet Hut, Steve McMillan, Simon Portegies Zwart, and many others (stellar dynamics and numerical methods); Kei Hiraki (GRAPE-DR and MN-Core); Ken Namura (GRAPE-6, GRAPE-DR, and MN-Core); Masaki Iwasawa, Ataru Tanikawa, Keigo Nitadori, Natsuki Hosono, Daisuke Namekata, and Kentaro Nomura (FDPS and related activities); Yutaka Ishikawa, Mitsuhisa Sato, Hirofumi Tomita, and many others (Fugaku development); Michiko Fujii, Takayuki Saito, Junko Kominami, and many others (stellar dynamics, galaxy formation, and planetary formation simulation on large-scale HPC platforms); Takayuki Muranushi and Youhei Ishihara (Formura DSL); many people from PFN (MN-Core); many people from PEZY Computing; and ExaScaler (PEZY-SC). I would like to thank all the people above. In addition, I'd like to thank Miyuki Tsubouchi, Yuko Wakamatsu, Yoshie Yamaguchi, Naoko Nakanishi, Yukiko Kimura, and Rika Ogawa for managing the projects I was involved. I would also like to thank the folks at Springer for making this book a reality. Finally, I thank my family, and in particular my partner, Yoko, for her continuous support.

Kobe, Japan   Junichiro Makino

Contents

Acronyms

ASIC	Application-specific integrated circuit
B/F	Bytes per flop
BB	Broadcast block
BM	Broadcast memory
CISC	Complex instruction-set computer
CG	Conjugate gradient (method)
CNN	Convolutional neural network
CPE	Computing processing element of sunway SW26010
DCTL	Direct coupled transistor logic
DEM	Distinct (or discrete) element method
DDM	Domain decomposition method
DDR	Double data rate (DRAM)
DMA	Direct memory access
DSL	Domain-specific language
EFGM	Element-free Galerkin method
FEM	Finite element method
FLOPS	Floating-point operations per second
FMA	Floating-point multiply and add
FMM	Fast multipole method
FPGA	Field-programmable gate array
FPU	Floating-point arithmetic unit
GaAs	Gallium arsenide
GPGPU	General-purpose computing on graphics processing units
HBM	High-bandwidth memory
HPC	High-performance computing
HPL	High-performance Linpack benchmark
ISA	Instruction-set architecture
MIMD	Multiple instruction streams, multiple data streams
MPE	Management processing element of sunway SW26010
MPS	Moving particle simulation
NUMA	Non-uniform memory access

OoO	Out-of-order (execution)
PCI	Peripheral component interconnect
PCIe	PCI express
PE	Processing element
RISC	Reduced instruction-set computer
SERDES	Serializer/deserializer
SIMD	Single instruction stream, multiple data dreams
SMT	Simultaneous multithreading
SPH	Smoothed particle hydrodynamics
SVE	Scalable vector extensions

Chapter 1
Introduction

Without theory, experience has no meaning.

— W. Edwards Deming

The purpose of this book is to provide the scientific basis of the design of processors for compute-intensive applications such as High-performance computing, deep neural networks and data sciences.

There are many textbooks on the design of computers. So a natural question is if there is any room for a new book. On the other hand, if we look at applications in the areas of high-performance computing or deep learning, the processors described in the standard textbooks are not main working horses. At the time of this writing, deep learning applications are mainly run on GPGPUs, and GPGPUs are also used in many compute-intensive applications. Also, the use of FPGAs for these applications have been an active research area for many years (in other words, the use of FPGA is still not mainstream in either fields). In addition, there are many startups developing processors for deep learning.

Practically all existing textbooks on computer architecture start with the design of ISA (instruction set architecture), and the range of processor architecture covered is rather narrow. It is essentially a multicore processor, each with pipelined superscalar processors with execution units with a small degree of SIMD parallelism. Multiple cores are connected through multiple levels of coherent data caches.

Such multicore designs have design tradeoffs within their design space, and they have been studied by many researchers and discussed in detail in textbooks. However, there are many possible architectures of processors not in this space, and the "optimal" designs for different architectures would be completely different.

In this book, we'll take a different approach. Instead of setting ISA as the basis of the computer architecture, we start from problems to be solved, and define "efficiency" as the measure of an architecture.

In the field of high-performance computing, the term "efficiency" is usually used to express the ratio between the achieved performance of an application program and the theoretical peak performance of the computer used, both measured in terms of the number of floating point operations per second.

© Springer Nature Switzerland AG 2021
J. Makino, *Principles of High-Performance Processor Design*,
https://doi.org/10.1007/978-3-030-76871-3_1

This "efficiency" is useful in some cases. For example, when we compare two programs which solve the same problem using the same numerical method, this efficiency is clearly a useful measure. The parallel efficiencies, both the so-called strong- and weak-scalings are also useful measures.

However, the efficiency in this form is not useful when we compare two programs which solve different problems on a same computer, or a same problem on two different computers. Is a program with 90% efficiency on an Intel Xeon processor better than a program with 50% efficiency on an NVIDIA GPGPU? How about a program with 60% efficiency on a Chinese or Japanese HPC processor?

Clearly, we need a more meaningful measure than the usual use of the word "efficiency". This lack of a meaningful or useful measure actually means something very strange about the research in computer architecture: We do not know the goal of our research.

Well, one would argue that we have been following the "quantitative" approach (e.g. [1]) for the last three or four decades, and that is certainly true. It is therefore important to summarize the structure of the "quantitative" approach.

How the "quantitative" approach works? It started with the analysis of how existing programs are executed on existing architectures. The classic example is the criticism on CISC ISA designed in 1970s. According to the famous review by Patterson and Ditzel [2], compilers at that time utilized only a small subset of instructions available on processors, and thus it would be much more efficient if we implement only those instructions that compilers could use efficiently. The idea of RISC was based on this consideration. As a result, RISC architecture in the early days shared the following characteristics:

(a) The load-store architecture, in which memory access is done through load and store instructions only and binary arithmetic operations takes two operands and one results, all in the register file.
(b) Fixed-stage pipeline.
(c) On-chip data cache which allows constant-delay memory access (when hit).

One important observation was that the arithmetic instructions which take memory operand should not be used since they generally result in long execution time and thus performance degradation. The latency of register-to-register operations are shorter than those for instructions with memory access. Thus, by separating the arithmetic operations and memory load and store, the compilers can utilize the processor resources more efficiently.

To be precise, the load-store architecture was invented in 1960s. The CDC 6600 [3] is the first well-known machine with the load-store architecture and three-address arithmetic instructions. It also has the superscalar architecture with register scoreboarding. First-generation RISC processors such as MIPS R2000/3000 and the first Sun SPARC processor did not have superscalar architecture. This is probably because it was still difficult to fit a microprocessor with superscalar architecture into a single die.

At least in late 1980s and early 1990s, these early RISC processors and their successors seemed to offer the performance much higher that that was available on a wide variety of CISC processors, including Intel 80x86, Motorola 680x0, DEC Vax and even IBM mainframes.

On the other hand, concerning the performance of numerical calculations, or floating-point operations, which is the main topic of this book, the difference between RISC and CISC processors were not so clear, since neither mainstream RISC processors nor CISC processors had fully pipelined floating-point units (FPUs). The floating-point performance of a microprocessor was determined primarily by the throughput of FPUs.

Thus, the relation between the so-called "quantitative" approach and the actual performance of microprocessors for HPC applications was not straightforward. The evolution of microprocessors from 1980s to 2020s would tell the consequence of the "quantitative" approach more clearly.

In 1989, Intel announced its i860 processor. It is the first microprocessor with a (almost) fully-pipelined floating-point unit. It could execute one double-precision floating-point addition in every cycle, and one double-precision floating-point multiplication in every two cycles. Even though i860 was not a great commercial success, many microprocessors followed it in integrating fully pipelined floating-point arithmetic units. These processors include HP PA-7100 (1992), DEC Alpha 21064 (1992), and Intel Pentium (1993).

This integration of pipelined FPUs gave microprocessors a big boost in the floating-point performance, with the help of the increased clock speed. The performance of early RISC processors with external FPUs was typically a few Mflops for real applications. While these processors with integrated FPUs had the peak performance of 100Mflops or higher.

One simple reason why fully-pipelined FPUs were implemented in high-end microprocessors of early 1990s is that it had become possible to integrate a fully-pipelined FPU in a single chip by the end of 1980s. Before 1990, microprocessors had separate FPU chips, such as Intel x87, Motorola 68881/68882, MIPS R3010, Am29027 and Weitek 3167. Also, more specialized FPUs for signal-processing use were developed by companies like Analog Devices (ADSP 3201/3202), LSI Logic (64132/64133) and TI (8847). Up to this point, the evolution of single-chip microprocessors had closely followed the evolution of high-end supercomputers, with the time lag of about 20 years. The first supercomputer with fully pipelined floating-point multiplier was CDC 7600 first delivered in 1969.

In the case of supercomputers, shared-memory vector-parallel machines with 16–32 processors, such as Cray C90 and T90 and NEC SX-4, both first shipped in 1995, were very much the last species of their kind. Cray could not develop the successor of T90. NEC had already switched from shared-memory architecture to distributed-memory architecture with SX-4.

In the case of microprocessors, as of early 2020s the increase of the number of cores for high-end microprocessors might have reached an end. Intel Xeon still keeps UMA (Uniform Memory Access) architecture, while AMD switched to NUMA (Non-Uniform Memory Access) architecture even for one processor package with its EPYC processor range.

The evolutionary paths after the integration of fully pipelined floating-point multiplier are also very similar for supercomputers and microprocessors. Initially, performance improvement came mostly from higher clock speed and better architecture (more instruction-level parallelism). Eventually, multiple (superscalar) floating-point units, SIMD units, and multicores followed. The exact order in which these hardware-level parallelism are utilized are slightly different, but in both cases the "final" form had 16–32 processors with superscalar and/or SIMD floating-point units.

In the case of vector-parallel supercomputers, they were replaced by distributed-memory supercomputers. In the US, they were based on microprocessors with single fully-pipelined floating-point multipliers. For example, Cray announced their T3D line in 1993, IBM announced SP in 1993. Silicon Graphics announced Power Challenge in 1993. Intel had developed machines based on their i860 processors, Touchstone Delta and Intel Paragon. Intel terminated the development of its i860 line of processors around 1995. Thus, the last big machine developped by Intel was ASCI Red, a one-off machine with around 9000 Pentium Pro processors.

In Japan, what happened was quite different, since both Fujitsu and NEC continued the development of vector processors, but with the distributed memory architecture. The first of this kind is Fujitsu VPP500. It is a commercial version of Numerical Wind Tunnel (NWT) [4], a machine developed following the specification of National Aeronautical Laboratory of Japan. NWT/VPP500 had a unique architecture in which up to 256 vector processor nodes are connected by a single big crossbar switch with quite high bandwidth. VPP500 was a great commercial success, and Fujitsu continued the development of distributed-memory vector-parallel machines until 2002, when they finally announced an HPC machine based on their SPARC64 microprocessor. As of the time of this writing, NEC is still developing vector-parallel machines.

Right now, almost all large HPC machines are based on either Intel Xeon processors or NVIDIA GPGPUs, with a few exceptions of Japanese and Chinese machines. However, as we have discussed, single-chip microprocessors are now at the same point as shared-memory vector processors were in early 1990s. We do not have very clear idea about what will come next.

The goal of this book is not to give the answer to the question of "what will come next", but to better understand the relationship between the underlying device technology and architecture, and to present a truly "quantitative" approach for the design of HPC systems.

The basic idea here is to define the minimum necessary energy for each applications, and define the efficiency of one architecture by the ratio between this minimum energy and its actual energy consumption.

This approach is inspired by the definition of the efficiency of thermal engines or the discrimination of pressure drag, frictional drag and induced drag of airplanes. In both cases, the efficiency is defined in terms of the ratio between the theoretical limit and actual value.

There has been no such definition of "efficiency" in the field of computer architecture. Recent developments of processor architecture, however, are very strongly motivated by the energy efficiency, since, for many years, the power consumption has been the primary limiting factor of the processor performance. This means that, we have been trying to design energy-efficient processors, without knowing how to do so and how far we can go.

In this book, We will first define how far we can go, and then discuss how we can approach there.

References

1. J. Hennessy, D. Patterson, *Computer Architecture: A Quantitative Approach* (Morgan Kaufmann, San Francisco, 1990)
2. D.A. Patterson, D.R. Ditzel, SIGARCH Comput. Archit. News **8**(6), 25–33 (1980). https://doi.org/10.1145/641914.641917
3. J.E. Thornton, *Design of a Computer the Control Data 6600* (Scott, Foresman and Company, Glenvew, 1970)
4. H. Miyoshi, M. Fukuda, T. Iwamiya, T. Takamura, M. Tuchiya, M. Yoshida, K. Yamamoto, Y. Yamamoto, S. Ogawa, Y. Matsuo, T. Yamane, M. Takamura, M. Ikeda, S. Okada, Y. Sakamoto, T. Kitamura, H. Hatama, M. Kishimoto, in *Supercomputing '94:Proceedings of the 1994 ACM/IEEE Conference on Supercomputing* (1994), pp. 685–692. https://doi.org/10.1109/SUPERC.1994.344334

Chapter 2
Traditional Approaches and Their Limitations

*Computer architectures have evolved to optimally exploit the
underlying hardware and software technologies to achieve
increasing levels of performance.*

— R. D. Groves

2.1 History

2.1.1 CDC 6600 and 7600

There have been a long and complicated discussion about the first digital computer,
but almost everybody would agree that the first supercomputer is either CDC
6600 [1] or Cray-1 [2], both designed by Seymour Cray. CDC 6600 is the first
machine with the load-store architecture and multiple execution units controlled
with register scoreboarding.

From the point of view of the structure of the floating-point unit, actually the
CDC 7600, which was also designed by Seymour Cray after 6600 and before Cray-
1, is more important, since it is the first machine with fully pipelined floating-point
multiplier. CDC 6600 had one floating-point add unit, two floating-point multiply
units, and one floating-point division unit. Though they can operate in parallel,
they are not fully pipelined, and require multiple cycles to finish one operation and
during the execution they do not accept operands for the next operation. With 7600,
multiple arithmetic units were replaced with a single, fully pipelined unit. Thus both
of the floating-point multiplier and adder could accept new operands and generate
one result at every clock cycle.

Thus, even though the performance is much higher, CDC 7600 had the architecture much simpler compared to that of CDC 6600, with fewer number of execution
units.

Here, it is important to look into more details of CDC 6600 and 7600, since
they have many of the features of modern high-performance processors, except
those related to SIMD operation units, multicores and multi-level caches. Most

© Springer Nature Switzerland AG 2021
J. Makino, *Principles of High-Performance Processor Design*,
https://doi.org/10.1007/978-3-030-76871-3_2

importantly, they have register scoreboarding mechanism, allowing multiple function units to operate in parallel. The same idea is used in almost all microprocessors today.

The basic idea of register scoreboarding is to allow the initiation of multiple instructions as early as possible. Consider the sequence in Listing 2.1. Here, for simplicity we assume all variables are in the register file, and each statement are translated to one instruction.

Listing 2.1 Example of reduction

```
1    X5  =  X1+X2
2    X6  =  X3+X4
3    X7  =  X5+X6
```

If this sequence of instructions is intended to obtain the reduction $X_1 + X_2 + X_3 + X_4$, that means instruction 3 need to wait the completion of instructions 1 and 2. On the other hand, instruction 2 can start before the completion of 1, since the result of instruction 1 is not used by instruction 2. Note that this is of course one natural way to define the semantics for the sequence of instructions. The simplest processor would execute the sequence of instructions one-by-one. Such a processor first reads registers X1 and X2, then adds them, then stores the result to X5, and only after the content of X5 is actually updated, instruction 2 is started.

If a single instruction, in particular the floating-point multiplication, takes many cycles to complete, this simplest design is actually not too bad, since the number of cycles not used for the execution of the multiplication instruction would be small. However, one obvious way to improve the performance of processors is to reduce the number of cycles required to perform the floating-point multiplication, and the fully pipelined unit of CDC 7600 gives the highest throughput of one result per clock cycle.

If we use a fully-pipelined unit with the above simple processor in which one instruction waits until the previous one finishes, it is clear that the pipelined unit is under-utilized. In order to make full use of a pipelined unit, the control logic should issue new instruction at every clock period. There are two possible approaches for this. One is to initiate instructions at every cycle as specified in the program, irrespective of the possible dependency problems. In this case, the compiler has to take care of the dependencies. In the above example, if the latency of the instruction is four. the compiler has to generate the code in Listing 2.2

Listing 2.2 Example of reduction with explicit delay

```
1    X5  =  X1+X2
2    X6  =  X3+X4
3    NOP
4    NOP
5    NOP
6    X7  =  X5+X6
```

Here, we define the word latency as follows. If the result of the instruction issued at cycle n is available to that at cycle $n + p$ but not at cycle $n + p - 1$, the latency is p.

The advantage of this approach is the simplicity of the hardware design. As far as we consider just one arithmetic unit, this approach can make full use of it when combined with a clever compiler (if the original problem and the source code are suitable). Thus, some of the early RISC processor, in particular the MIPS processor, used this approach, and its name, Microprocessor without interlocked pipeline stages, clearly indicates the approach used. However, this approach works only if one instruction is issued per clock cycle.

In examples above, we assumed that the storage locations Xn are registers. In the actual code we of course have the data in the main memory, and before issuing the actual arithmetic operation, data should be loaded into registers, and the result should then be stored to the main memory. Consider a simple loop of vector operation

$$\mathbf{c} = \mathbf{a} + \mathbf{b}, \tag{2.1}$$

in C language of Listing 2.3.

Listing 2.3 Example of a vector operation

```
for (int i=0, i<n;i++) c[i] = a[i]+b[i];
```

Since both the CDC machines and early MIPS processors had the load-store architecture, for each addition operation we need the following four instructions

1. load one element of **a**
2. load one element of **b**
3. add the loaded two elements
4. store the result to the location of the element of **c**

If the processor can issue (and execute) only one instruction per cycle, even if the arithmetic unit is fully pipelined, the efficiency of the calculation code would be rather low. Thus, we can see that if we have load-store architecture, it is necessary that the processor can issue and execute multiple instructions per cycle in order to make full use of the pipelined arithmetic unit. In the case of CDC 6600, arithmetic units are not yet fully pipelined. Even so. it had multiple arithmetic units as well as load-store units. Thus, in order to make efficient use of these multiple function units, it was necessary to use the idea of register scoreboarding. Let us now go back to the original Listing 2.1. With the register scoreboarding, it becomes possible to issue instructions which use the result of yet-to-be-finished previous instructions, since the scoreboarding logic let the instruction wait until the result becomes available. The scoreboarding logic takes care of other kind of resource conflicts, and thus allows efficient use of multiple function units.

Let us discuss how this simple loop is executed in some more details. this loop would be compiled to something like Listing 2.4

Listing 2.4 Scalar instructions for a simple loop

```
1   I=0
2   R1 = M1[I]
3   R2 = M2[I]
4   R3 = R1+R2
5   M3[I] =R3
6   I+= 1
7   IF I<63 GOTO 2
```

If we have a simple scalar CPU which executes Listing 2.4 step by step, the calculation speed will be very low. Addition (3) has to wait the completion of load(2), and store(5) has to wait add(4). Conditional jump(7) has to wait the increment(6). Let us assume that the result of load instruction can be used after two cycles and addition also two cycles, and two load instructions, one addition, one integer increments, one floating-point addition, and one store can all be issued and executed in parallel, and that we can issue up to four instructions per cycle. Thus two load instructions are issued in the first cycle in the loop, and then addition, and then store. The execution of addition starts at cycle 3, and store at cycle 5. If we neglect the cycles for inclement and branch, the next loop iteration can start at cycle 5, when the use of registers R1 and R2 are finished. Thus, one loop iteration requires four cycles, and the actual addition is performed only once in every four cycles. This is certainly not ideal.

One possibile way to improve the performance is the loop unrolling as shown in Listing 2.5. After some reordering, this loop can be executed as shown in Listing 2.6. The rescheduling can be done either by software or by hardware (out-of-order or "OoO" execution) or both.

Listing 2.5 4-times unrolled instructions for a simple loop

```
1  I=0
2   R1 = M1[I]
3   R4 = M1[I+1]
4   R7 = M1[I+2]
5   R10 = M1[I+3]
6   R2 = M2[I]
7   R5 = M2[I+1]
8   R8 = M2[I+2]
9   R11 = M2[I+3]
10   R3 = R1+R2
11   R6 = R4+R5
12   R9 = R7+R8
13   R12 = R10+R11
14   M3[I] =R3
15   M3[I+1] =R6
```

```
16   M3[I+2] =R9
17   M3[I+3] =R12
18   I+= 4
19   IF I<63 GOTO 2
```

Listing 2.6 4-times unrolled and rescheduled instructions for a simple loop

```
1  I=0
2    R1 = M1[I];     R2 = M2[I]
3    R4 = M1[I+1]; R5 = M2[I+1]
4    R7 = M1[I+2]; R8 = M2[I+2];   R3 = R1+R2
5    R10 = M1[I+3]; R11 = M2[I+3] R6 = R4+R5
6    R9 = R7+R8; M3[I] =R3
7    R12 = R10+R11; M3[I+1] =R6
8    M3[I+2] =R9
9    M3[I+3] =R12
10   I+= 4
11   IF I<63 GOTO 2
```

Note that in Listing 2.6, the line numbers denote the cycle count at which the execution of the instruction actually start. We can see that now the loop body is eight cycles. Thus, we have improved the efficiency from 25 to 50%. With more unrolling, the efficiency would approach to 100%.

One problem with this unrolling approach is that we need a large number of registers. Both CDC 6600 and 7600 had only eight registers, and most of modern machines have 32 registers visible in the instruction set. With eight registers, we can unroll the above simple loop only two times, and the efficiency we can achieve would be very limited. We can resolve this problem by the technique known as register renaming. Consider the instruction sequence in Listing 2.7. Instruction 6 need to wait the completion of instruction 4. Thus, execution sequence would look like Listing 2.8.

Listing 2.7 multiple loop body

```
2    R1 = M1[I]
3    R2 = M2[I]
4    R3 = R1+R2
5    M3[I] =R3
6    R1 = M1[I+1]
7    R2 = M2[I+1]
8    R3 = R1+R2
9    M3[I+1] =R3
10   R1 = M1[I+2]
11   R2 = M2[I+2]
12   R3 = R1+R2
13   M3[I+2] =R3
14   R1 = M1[I+3]
15   R2 = M2[I+3]
16   R3 = R1+R2
17   M3[I+3] =R3
```

Listing 2.8 multiple loop body execution

```
2   R1 = M1[I];     R2 = M2[I]
3
4   R3 = R1+R2
5
6   M3[I] =R3;   R1 = M1[I+1];   R2 = M2[I+1]
7
8   R3 = R1+R2
9
10  M3[I+1] =R3;     R1 = M1[I+2];   R2 = M2[I+2]
10
11  R3 = R1+R2
12
13  M3[I+2] =R3;   R1 = M1[I+3];   R2 = M2[I+3]
14
15  R3 = R1+R2
16
17  M3[I+3] =R3
```

The basic idea of register renaming is to make the physical number of registers larger than that specified by the instruction set (architecture registers), and to maintain a mapping table between architecture and physical registers. For actual mechanism of mapping, see any decent book on computer architecture. The idea is that the execution can now proceed as shown in Listing 2.9. Here the notation Rx(Py) means the architecture register x mapped to physical register y.

Listing 2.9 multiple loop body execution with renaming

```
2   R1(P1) = M1[I];     R2(P2) = M2[I]
3   R1(P3) = M1[I+1];   R2(P4) = M2[I+1]
4   R3(P5) = R1(P1)+R2(P2); R1(P6) = M1[I+2];   R2(P7) = M2[I+2]
5   R3(P8) = R1(P3)+R2(P4); R1(P9) = M1[I+3];   R2(P10) = M2[I+3]
6   M3[I] =R3(P5);   R3(P1) = R1(P6)+R2(P7)
7   M3[I+1] =R3(P8);   R3(P2) = R1(P9)+R2(P10)
8   M3[I+2] =R3(P1)
9   M3[I+3] =R3(P2)
```

In this example, in cycles 4 and 5 two loads and one add are started, and in cycles 6 and 7 one add and one store. If we can perform the register renaming and rescheduling further on for larger number of operations, we will have cycles where two loads, one add, and one store are started, and that means the best possible performance is achieved.

Note that with this register renaming, in principle we can improve the performance of one program, written in one instruction set, by changing the processor hardware. For example, by increasing the number of functional units and the number of instructions issued per clock. This approach has been the most important way to improve the performance of modern microprocessors for the last 30 years.

On the other hand, in the above example, we need 10 physical registers, which is more than three times the number of architecture registers used, to fully hide the latencies of operations, even though the assumed latencies are very small. In addition, before the first store is started, eight loads have been started. Thus, around 20 instructions should be re-scheduled at run time. The actual latencies are much larger and in many cases the loop body contains many more instructions. Thus, for this approach to be really useful, the number of physical registers and the number of instructions to be rescheduled must be very large, such as more than one hundred. In fact, some of modern high-end microprocessors do have such a large buffer (reorder buffer) for instructions and a large number of physical registers.

However, at the time of CDC 7600, it was not practical to design a processor with such a large a number of physical registers and a large enough reorder buffer. Cray adopted a very different approach to design his new machine, Cray-1. In Sect. 2.1.2 we will look at Cray-1.

2.1.2 Cray-1

As in the case of CDC 7600. Cray-1 (Fig. 2.1) has the fully pipelined floating-point arithmetic units. Thus the difference in the peak performance came mainly from the improved clock frequency. CDC 7600 operated on 36.4 MHz clock and Cray-1 on 80 MHz. However, a much larger improvement of the actual application performance came from the addition of the new "vector" instruction set and corresponding register set. The vector instructions of Cray-1 operate on "vectors" of length up to 64. Thus, a single vector load instruction loads up to 64 values to a vector register. Vector arithmetic instructions are applied to registers, and vector store instructions move data from a vector register to the main memory. These vector instructions makes it possible to achieve near-peak performance with relatively simple hardware and software. Compared with the complex logic necessary to implement register scoreboarding, renaming and reorder buffer, logic circuit to implement vector instructions is much simpler. We do not need scoreboard, and instructions can be executed in-order, with the issue frequency much less than one per clock cycle.

The vector instruction sequence for the simple addition of two vectors would be expressed as Listing 2.10.

Listing 2.10 Vector instructions for a simple loop

```
1   VR1 = M1[0..63]
2   VR2 = M2[0..63]
3   VR3 = VR1+VR2
4   M3[0..63] =VR3
```

We have seen that a superscalar CPU with instruction reorder (out-of-order execution) could achieve essentially the same near-peak performance for the above loop, but it requires much larger hardware resources.

The total gate count of Cray-1 is around 230k gates, and floating point addition, multiplication, and reciprocal units use 53k gates, or around 23% of the total gate count. If we use the usual conversion of 4 transistors per gate, we can say that Cray-1 is made of around 1M transistors, for one fully functional floating-point units. This number is quite small compared to the number of transistors used per one FPU in

Fig. 2.1 The Cray-1 Supercomputer with its main designer, Seymour Cray. URL: https://www.chessprogramming.org/File:Cray1Seymour.jpg Author: Gerd Isenberg This file is licensed under the Creative Commons Attribution-ShareAlike 3.0 Unported (CC BY-SA 3.0)

microprocessors. In Table 2.1 we show the number of transistors per one FPU of Cray-1 compared with that of several representative processors.

A large fraction of transistors of microprocessors are used for cache memories and thus not for the processor core itself. So one can argue that this comparison is somewhat unfair. On the other hand, even when we assume that around half of the total transistors are used for cache memories, there is still the difference of nearly an order of magnitude. The Knights Landing processor comes closest to Cray-1, but it is known to be extremely difficult to use and the development of its successor, Knights Hill, was canceled. Moreover, in order to increase the peak performance per core, Intel processors after Pentium 4 have added more and more FPUs per

Table 2.1 Year of
introduction and number of
transistors per one FPU of
representative processors

Processor	Year	# of transistors per FPU
Cray-1	1976	900K
Earth simulator	2002	8M
NVIDIA fermi	2010	6M
Pentium 4	2000	42M
Sandy bridge	2011	70M
Haswell	2014	40M
Knights landing	2014	6.5M
Skylake	2017	18M

core, and both Knights Landing and Skylake have 8-way SIMD FPUs (two of them works as independent functional units). This expansion of the SIMD width results in the reduction of the total number of transistors per FPU, but at the same time causes serious degradation in the application efficiency.

Thus, it is probably not unfair to say that the vector architecture of Cray-1 made it possible to fully utilize its pipelined floating-point arithmetic unit with the circuit size around 1/10 or less compared to what is necessary to achieve a similar efficiency with superscalar, out-of-order architecture, even with SIMD functional units.

On the other hand, we all know that the Cray vector lines of supercomputers effectively ended with Cray C90 which was introduced in 1991. In 1980s, three Japanese computer companies, Hitachi, Fujitsu and NEC, started to sell their versions of vector supercomputers, but Hitachi shifted to microprocessor-based machines in 1996, and Fujitsu followed Hitachi in 2002. As of 2021, NEC is the only company in the world which still sells the machines with the vector architecture.

If the vector architecture is so much more efficient in the use of transistors compared to superscalar designs, why the switch from vector architecture to scalar architecture took place in 1990s?

If we take a look at the first edition of the famous and influential textbook "Computer Architecture: A Quantitative Approach" [3], we find interesting statements

Recent trends in vector machine design have focused on high peak-vector performance and multiprocessing. Meanwhile, high-speed scalar machines concentrate on keeping the ratio of peak to sustained performance near one. Thus, of the peak rates advance comparably, the sustained rates of the scalar machines will advance comparably, the sustained rates of the scalar machines will advance more quickly, and the scalar machines will continue to close the CPF gap.

The 1990s will be interesting as the pipelined scalar machines that exploit more instruction-level parallelism and are usually much cheaper (because their peak performance and hence total hardware is much less) begin to offer performance levels for many applications that are difficult to distinguish from those of vector machines.

This is the prediction made in 1990, when Cray and Japanese computer companies were all selling their vector processors, and now we know that this is very much what actually happened.

As will be discussed later, the architecture of CDC 7600 and and that of "the pipelined scalar machines that exploit more instruction-level parallelism", at the

time when the the the above text was written, such as IBM Power, Sun SuperSparc and
MIPS 10K are quite similar. Thus, one might think that the vector architecture of
Cray-1 is largely a result of a misconception which happened to prevail only until
the better solution was (re)-invented.

In order to understand what really happened, we should look at the building
blocks of machines. The logic circuits of CDC 7600 was made of discrete
transistors, and it has a fully pipelined 60-bit floating-point unit running at the clock
frequency of 36.4 MHz. The primary memory of CDC 7600 (small core memory,
SCM) consists of 32 banks of magnetic-core memory modules, with 60-bit data
width and the cycle time of 275 ns. Because of the long cycle time of the magnetic
core memory, a large number of memory banks were necessary to serve the need
of CPU, and even so, a very large number of outstanding load instructions are
necessary to execute a simple loop like

```
for(int i=0;i<63:i++)  c[i]=a[i]+b[i];
```

The fact that the cycle time of the memory is 10 times that of the clock period
of the machine means that it would take at least 10 cycles before the result of a
load instruction becomes available to the subsequent instructions. Thus, without the
techniques such as out-of-order execution, loop unrolling and register renaming, the
above simple loop would require more than 20 clock cycles per addition, resulting
in less than 5% of the peak performance.

To make the matter even more complicated, CDC 7600 has a two-level memory
hierarchy of the primary and secondary memories. The secondary memory (large
core memory, LCM) is an eight-bank memory with the 8-word width and the cycle
time of 1760 ns. Thus, SCM and LCM look like the data cache and the main memory
of modern machines, but in CDC 7600 the data transfer between SCM and LCM
need to be controlled by software.

The memory organization and relative speed of CPU, fast small memory and
slow large memory of CDC 7600 and those of high-performance microprocessors
in early 1990s are not much different. The large main memory has very long cycle
time compared to the CPU clock period, and thus we need a fast memory with
shorter cycle time between CPU and main memory.

However, the memory organization of Cray-1 is completely different. The cycle
time of Cray-1 CPU is 12.5 ns. The cycle time of its main memory, consisting of
SRAM chips, is 50 ns, and the entire 1M words of the main memory is made of
fast SRAM chips. Thus, the user program of Cray-1 can access anywhere in the
main memory with the latency 1/30 of that of CDC 7600, while the CPU cycle time
is improved by roughly a factor of two. Thus, for Cray-1, there is no need for the
cache or small and fast memory. The main memory of Cray-1 is as fast as the L2
cache memory of modern microprocessors. Moreover, the bandwidth of the main
memory of Cray-1 (and its successor, Cray X-MP) is extraordinarily high.

We can see that the switch from the two-level memory hierarchy of CDC 7600
to single-level main memory of Cray-1 was made possible by the switch from the
magnetic core memory to SRAM chips. This switch resulted in both much higher
bandwidth and much lower latency.

As we have already seen, the primary advantage of the vector architecture over superscalar architecture with similar throughput is the required number of transistors. Cray-1 required around 1/20 transistors per floating-point arithmetic unit compared to a modern processor, Intel Skylake, even though the Skylake is the most transistor-efficient in the series of Intel processors after Pentium 4, except for the (failed) Knights Landing processor.

Well, if the vector architecture is so much more transistor-efficient than the superscalar architecture, why the latter replaced the former in 1990s?

To answer this question, we need to understand the evolution tracks of these two architectures. In the following sections, we summarize the history of machines with vector architectures and superscalar microprocessors.

2.1.3 The Evolution of Vector Processors

Table 2.2 shows the numbers of processing elements (PE), the numbers of pipelines per PE, and the clock frequencies of supercomputers with vector architectures from main players: Cray, Control Data and three Japanese companies, Hitachi,

Table 2.2 List of major vector machines

Machine	Year of introduction	# of PEs	# of pipelines per PE	Clock (MHz)
Cray-1	1976	1	1	80
Cyber 205	1981	1	4	50
Cray X-MP	1982	4	1	105
Fujitsu VP-200	1982	1	2	125
Hitac S-810	1983	1	4	71.4
Cray-2	1985	4	1	243
NEC SX-2	1985	1	4	167
Cray Y-MP	1988	8	1	167
Hitac S-820	1988	1	4	250
Fujitsu VP2600	1989	1	8	312.5
NEC SX-3	1989?	4	4	345
Cray C90	1991	16	2	244
Cray T90	1995	32	2	450
Hitac S-3800	1993	4	8	500
NEC SX-4	1994	32	8	125
Fujitsu VPP500	1993	140	8	100
Fujitsu VPP5000	1999	140	16	300
NEC ES(SX-6)	2001	5120	8	500
NEC SX-8	2005	?	4	2000
NEC SX-9	2008	16	16	3200
NEC SX-Aurora	2017	?	96	1600

Fujitsu and NEC. Machines from Cray-1 to NEC SX-4 are either uniprocessor machines or shared-memory multiprocessors. Fujitsu VPP500 to NEC SX-Aurora are distributed-memory machines. We do not list ETA-10, which was designed as an 8-processor shared-memory machine and shipped in 1987, since its "shared memory" never really worked. We consider a set of add and multiply pipelines as "one pipeline".

We can see that the increase of all of the three numbers shown in Table 2.2 are rather modest for the shared-memory machines. The last shared-memory vector machine from Cray, the T90, has 64 pipelines in total, with clock speed only 6 times higher than that of Cray-1. It is true that Seymour Cray himself was working on Cray-3 and Cray-4, each with the clock frequency of 500 MHz and 1 GHz, but only a small number of prototypes were made. As a result, the increase in the peak performance had been rather modest, from 160 Mflops of Cray-1 to 32 Gflops of Cray T90, or 64 Gflops of NEC NEC SX-4, in 19 years. This is a factor of 200–400, and is much smaller than the usual trend of a factor of 100 per decade, which would result in the performance close to 1 Tflops by 1995.

Cray-1 had one processor with one add pipeline and one multiply pipeline. Thus, it has the smallest possible configuration of a pipelined vector processor. The successors of Cray-1 and their competitor evolved in three directions:

(a) Clock frequency
(b) Number of pipelines per processor
(c) Number of processors

In the following, we will discuss what were the limiting factors for each of these three directions.

Let us first discuss the clock frequency. Very roughly, if the processor logic itself is implemented using multiple logic board, as in the case of Cray vector-parallel machines, it is very difficult to make the clock frequency higher than 500 MHz. In fact, even when the processor is integrated into single logic board, it is still difficult to make the clock frequency higher than 500 MHz. Only with NEC SX-8, which has the processor integrated into a single CMOS VLSI, the clock speed of vector processors exceeded 1 GHz. Quite interestingly, the clock speed of NEC CMOS vector processors reached the peak with SX-9, and had become lower on newer machines. However, here the limiting factor is not the signal delay but the power consumption, as we'll discuss later. For shared-memory vector-parallel machines, the main limiting factor for the clock speed is simply the physical distance between the processor logic and memory units.

Let us now discuss the number of pipelines and the number of processors. NEC SX-4 and SX-9 had 256 pipelines connected to one physically shared memory, and there are no other machines with the number of pipelines larger than 512, except for SX-Aurora which we will discuss in more details later. SX-Aurora is quite different from its predecessors because its relative memory bandwidth is quite small. SX-4 was still competitive with other machines, in particular Fujitsu VPP500, while SX-9 was not. The peak performance of the single node of SX-4 was two times higher than that of Cray T90. On the other hand, the memory bandwidth of single-node SX-4 was 512 GB/s, and that of T90 was 350 GB/s. Thus, the difference in the memory bandwidth was rather small. We argue that 512 GB/s was close to the limit of the data transfer rate for shared-memory vector parallel machines in 1995, and that these machines were marginally competitive. This means the hardware cost of the physically shared memory with the bandwidth of 512 GB/s was pretty high in 1995.

When we compare the shared-memory vector machines and distributed-memory vector machines, it is clear that the shared-memory architecture itself had been the main bottleneck for the performance improvement of the former machines. In 1995, Cray T90 could integrate only 32 processors or 64 pipelines, while in 1993 Fujitsu VPP500 had already integrated more than 1328 pipelines (with an actually installed 166-PE system). Since the clock frequency of VPP500 was 4.5 times lower than that of T90, the actual peak performance was different by a factor around five, not 20, but even so it was clear that T90 was an dead end of the evolution of an architecture. The total memory bandwidth of the 166-PE NAL NWT (with 9.5 ns clock cycle) was 2241 GB/s (13.5 GB/s per PE), while that of T90 was 350 GB/s. The 166 PEs of NAL NWT were connected with a crossbar switch with the total bandwidth of 117.88 GB/s (421 MB/s per PE per direction). Thus we can conclude that, by limiting the connection bandwidth between PEs to 1/16 of that of the local memory bandwidth, the designers of Fujitsu VPP500 had succeeded to increase the number of processors beyond 32, which was the effective physical limit for shared-memory vector processors.

Up to the time of ES, the designers of parallel vector machines tried to keep the ratio between the main memory bandwidth and floating-point arithmetic operation throughput constant. This number is usually called as B/F or bytes per flop. The B/F number of Cray-1 was 4, since it performed two arithmetic operations (add and multiply) and one load or one store operation per clock cycle. Cyber 205 had the B/F number of 12, since its memory-to-memory instruction required that two load and one store operations were performed per clock cycle per arithmetic pipeline. NEC has been reducing the B/F number gradually, from 8 of machines up to SX-4 to 4 of ES, and to 2.5 of SX-9 to 0.55 of SX-Aurora.

This B/F number has two important implications.

1. On machines with high B/F numbers, simple programs, compiled with simple compilers. can achieve very high efficiency.
2. On the other hand, as the semiconductor technology advances, keeping high B/F number has become more and more expensive.

In the extreme case of B/F = 12, a simple vector addition expressed as
```
for(int i=0;i<n:i++)  c[i]=a[i]+b[i];
```
can achieve 50% of the theoretical peak (50% because only the addition is performed). Thus, any program which operates on long vectors (a large number of freedoms) can achieve the efficiency of 50% or higher, if the memory access pattern is regular.

Of course, not all memory access patterns are regular. Many real-world applications use irregular or nested grids. In the case of the irregular grid, there are many different methods to store data, but in any method, we need to access the data through "indirect addressing", with the loops of the forms

```
for(int i=0;i<n;i++) b[i]=a[idex[i]];
```
(gather operation), and

```
for(int i=0;i<n;i++) b[idex[i]]=a[i];
```
(scatter operation).

The original Cray-1 did not have the hardware support of these gather/scatter operations, but Cray-1S and later Cray vector machines all had the support of gather/scatter. The throughput of gather/scatter operations on vector processors were lower than that of regular load/store, but not by a huge factor in the case of vector processors with a small number of arithmetic pipelines. As in the case of Cray-1, the main memory consisted of multiple banks. Thus, except for the extreme cases where the accesses are concentrated to a small number of banks, the memory system of Cray-1S and later could provide reasonable throughput even for gather/scatter operations.

This very large memory bandwidth and the capability of gather/scatter made it possible to achieve high efficiency (around 50%) for many applications. On the other hand, we should note that this high memory bandwidth was practical only in the time window of 1970–1990, where the SRAM memory replaced the magnetic core memory and yet a single processor was constructed using multiple LSI chips. The former means the I/O bandwidth of a single SRAM chip is very high compared to its capacity, and the latter means the cost of chip-to-chip connections for processor-memory communication is not very high since there are already a very large number of wires for chip-to-chip connections to implement a processor.

In other words, once the silicon VLSI technology had reached the point that single processor could be integrated into a single chip, keeping a high memory bandwidth to external memory chips had become very difficult, and with the further advance of the silicon VLSI technology it just became even more difficult. As the silicon VLSI technology advances, the physical size of a transistor becomes smaller, and the power consumption per switching becomes smaller. In addition, the average length of wires between transistors becomes smaller, also resulting in smaller power consumption. On the other hand, it is not easy to reduce the power consumption associated with moving data between processor chip and memory chip, since the wire length between LSIs, and also the length of the wires within the chips, cannot be reduced easily. The primary method to reduce the power consumption has been reducing the I/O voltage. The I/O voltage of DRAM memory has been reduced from 2.5 V of DDR to 1.2 V of DDR4, and to 1.1 V of DDR5. The I/O voltage is reduced to 0.5 V in the case of LPDDR5. Since the power consumption is proportional to the square of the I/O voltage, this reduction is quite effective, but not enough to support the increase of the memory bandwidth necessary to keep the B/F number high.

2.1.4 Lessons from the History of Vector-Parallel Architecture

We summarize the main points we learned from the history of vector-parallel machines as follows

- Vector architecture with high B/F numbers made the development of high-performance applications relatively easy.
- High B/F numbers to external main memory were possible only in the time window of 1970–1990.
- Thus, machines with traditional vector architecture in year 2000 or later were not the most cost-effective machines.

In the next subsection, we will see the evolution of single-chip processors.

2.1.5 The Evolution of Single-Chip Processors

Table 2.3 shows some of the representative microprocessors used in large HPC systems, again with the clock frequency in MHz, the numbers of cores and floating-point pipelines per core. If we compare Tables 2.2 and 2.3, we can see the trends are largely similar with one difference. The increase in the clock frequency for microprocessors (around a factor of 100) is much higher than that for shared-memory vector processors (around a factor of six). The number of pipelines per core reached 16 in both cases, and the number of cores also reached numbers around 32 (72 for the case of Intel Xeon Phi, which was not a great commercial success resulting in the cancellation of the project).

The increase of the clock speed is much larger partly because the move to designs with deeper pipelines, but partly because of the so-called CMOS scaling law, or Dennard's law. The CMOS scaling means that, if the physical size of the transistor is reduced by a factor of k, by reducing the supply voltage by a same factor of k and increasing the concentration of impurity by a factor of k, we can increase the switching speed of the transistor by a factor of k, while reducing the switching power by k^3.

As far as this "law" works, the reduction in the transistor size by a factor of two should give the performance improvement of a factor of eight, at the same power consumption and the same silicon area. With the transistor size halved, we can put four times more transistors, each of which can operate two times faster.

This "law" is applicable to CMOS design rules larger than around 90 nm or supply voltage higher than around 1 V, which were reached in early 2000s. Since then, the reduction in the transistor size did not automatically lead to the reduction in the supply voltage. As of 2021, even with the high-end fabrication technology such as TSMC N7 (not really 7 nm design rule), the standard supply voltage is 0.65 V. This is because the switching operation of a CMOS device requires that the operating voltage is higher than the threshold voltage (around 0.3 V), and as supply voltage approaches this limit the switching speed becomes slower.

Figure 2.2 shows the clock frequencies of the microprocessors listed in Table 2.3. We can see that the clock frequency increased from 25 MHz of Intel i860 (1989) to 1.7 GHz of Intel Xeon (Foster, 2001) by a factor of 68 in 12 years, and after that there has been essentially no increase until 2021. Actually, we can see that the clock frequency has been gradually decreasing since 2007. This change in early 2000s is due to the lower limit in the operating voltage. To be more precise, the increase of the clock speed by a factor of 68 in the period of 1989–2001 is much larger than what we can expect from Dennard's law, since the shrink in the one-dimensional size of the transistor is only by about a factor of ten. There are two main reasons for this very large increase in the clock frequency:

(a) High supply voltage is used to keep switching speed high.
(b) deeply pipelined superscalar microarchitectures have been adopted to allow higher clock frequency.

Table 2.3 List of major single-chip processors used in large HPC systems

Chip	Year of introduction	clock	# of cores	# pipes per core	peak Gflops
Intel i860	1989	25	1	0.75	0.0375
(CM-5 VPU)	1992	32	1	2	128
DEC Alpha 21064	1992	150	1	0.5	0.15
DEC Alpha 21164	1995	266	1	1	0.532
Intel Pentium Pro	1995	150	1	0.5	0.2
IBM PowerPC 604e	1996	200	1	0.5	0.375
IBM Power4	2001	1100	2	2	8.800
Intel Xeon 1.7 GHz	2001	1700	1	1	3.4
AMD Opteron 140	2003	1400	1	1	2.8
AMD Opteron 180	2005	2400	2	1	9.6
Intel Xeon 5080	2006	1700	2	1	6.8
Intel Xeon 5160	2006	3000	2	1	12
Intel Xeon X3230	2007	2667	4	1	21
AMD Opteron 1356	2008	2000	4	2	32
Fujitsu SPARC64 VII	2008	2500	4	2	40
Intel Xeon X3470	2009	3070	4	2	49
Fujitsu SPARC64 VIIIfx	2010	2000	8	4	128
Intel Xeon E5-2470	2012	2300	8	4	147
Fujitsu SPARC64 XIfx	2014	2500	16 × 2	8	1280
Intel Xeon E5-2690v3	2014	2600	12	8	500
Intel Xeon Phi 7290	2016	(1500)	72	16	(3456)
Intel Xeon Platinum 8180	2017	(2500)	28	16	(2240)
Fujitsu A64fx	2019	2200	12 × 4	16	3379

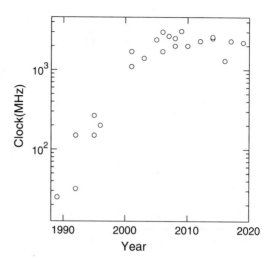

Fig. 2.2 The clock frequency of representative microprocessors used in large HPC systems plotted as a function of time

During the same period of 1989–2001, even though the clock frequency increased by nearly two orders of magnitude, the peak floating-point performance increased only by a factor around 200 (see Fig. 2.3). The highest improvement by 2001 was achieved not by the processor with the highest clock frequency (Xeon 1.7 GHz), but with lower clock and multiple cores/pipelines (IBM Power4). For the latter, the increase in the clock frequency over Intel i860 was by a factor of 44, and the increase in the floating point pipelines was by a factor of 5.3.

One very surprizing fact here is that the total number of transistors in one Intel i860 processor is around 1 million, while that of IBM Power4 is 174 million and that of Xeon 1.7 GHz is 42 million (Table 2.4). This means that the number of transistors used to implement one processor core has increased by a factor much larger than the factor at which the number of floating-point pipes per processor core increased, during the period of 1989–2001. After these processors, the number of transistors per floating-point unit reached the peak with 4-core processors like AMD Opteron 1536, and started to decrease. As of 2021, Intel Xeon Phi 7290 seems to use the smallest number of transistors per floating-point pipe among the processors after year 2000, and the number for Fujitsu A64Fx is close to that for Xeon Phi. Mainstream Xeon processor still uses nearly three times more transistors per floating point unit compared to Xeon Phi, or 20 times more compared to Intel i860.

In the case of shared-memory vector-parallel machines, the limiting factor for the performance was essentially the wires to connect processors and memory units. It seemed that to make 64 pipelines share one physical memory unit would result in high hardware cost, in particular when we want to keep high B/F numbers.

Table 2.4 Number of transistors and that of FP pipelines of some of major single-chip processors

Chip	# transistors	# pipes	# transistors/pipe
Intel i860	1M	0.75	1.3M
DEC Alpha 21164	9.3M	1	9.3M
Intel Xeon 1.7 GHz	44M	1	44M
IBM Power4	174M	4	44M
AMD Opteron 1356	758M	8	95M
Fujitsu SPARC64 VIIIfx	768M	16	48M
Intel Xeon Phi 7290	8G	1152	7M
Intel Xeon Platinum 8180	8G	448	19M
Fujitsu A64fx	8.8G	768	11.5M

Fig. 2.3 The theoretical peak performance of representative microprocessors used in large HPC systems plotted as a function of time

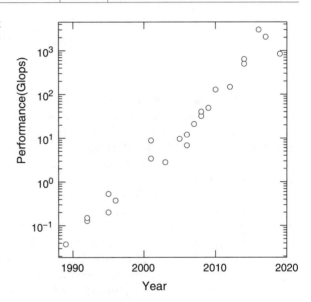

2.1.6   The Impact of Hierarchical Cache

Even though there seems to be similarity between Tables 2.2 and 2.3, the B/F numbers are very different. In the case of shared-memory vector-parallel processors, B/F numbers are at least four. On the other hand, on single-chip microprocessors, the B/F numbers are much smaller. Intel i860 had B/F = 4, but this number gradually decreased to around 0.1 of Xeon Platinum. Fujitsu A64fx has much higher B/F of around 0.35. However, even so, this number is less than one tenths of that of Intel i860.

This difference comes from the fact that with the modern single-chip microprocessors, the main memory is still external. Thus, the communication bandwidth between the processor chip and memory chips is limited by the number and length of the wires, and is much lower than the total floating-point performance of the chip.

Another difference in the architecture is that the memory system of these single-chip microprocessors are cache-based. Most of processors listed in Table 2.3 have L1 and L2 caches, and most of processors with four or larger number of processor cores have L3 caches. Here, Fujitsu processors are exceptions since all Fujitsu processors listed here have L1 and L2 caches but no L3 cache. Their L2 caches are shared by 8–16 cores. The L1 cache typically provides the B/F number of eight or four. Thus, if the application can make good use of the L1 cache, it is not impossible to achieve very high efficiency. However, usually L1 caches are very small (16–64 kB per core), and we have increasingly larger L2 and L3 caches, with decreasing bandwidth. There are two reasons why the bandwidth of L2 and L3 caches are smaller than that of the L1 cache. The first one is that they are physically more distant from processor cores than L1 caches are, and thus read and write operations take more power. The second reason is that they are physically shared by multiples cores and thus to increase the total bandwidth is difficult. These are exactly the same problems as we saw with the main memory of the shared-memory vector processors, but actually more difficult to solve because of the two-dimensional nature of a single-chip VLSI circuit.

Because of this structure of hierarchical caches with decreasing bandwidth, compared to shared-memory vector-parallel processors, modern multicore processors are far more difficult to use. Very roughly speaking, we could achieve a reasonable efficiency on shared-memory vector-parallel machines once the compute-intensive parts of the code are "vectorized". However, with modern multicore processors, vectorization alone would result in the efficiency of a few percents and at the best case around 10%, since the performance would be limited by the main memory bandwidth.

Of course, some operations can make good use of hierarchical caches. The most well-known example is probably the matrix-matrix multiplication

$$A = B \cdot C + D, \tag{2.2}$$

where A and D are matrices of size $m \times n$, B is that of size $m \times k$ and C $k \times n$. Here, the total operation count is $2mnk$, while if we can fit B or C into the on-chip cache, the amount of the main memory access can be reduced to $3mn + (m+n)k$. In this case, the necessary memory bandwidth, in terms of B/F number, is given by $12/k$. This is the maximum gain we can achieve through the cache blocking.

Even when the on-chip cache is much smaller, if it is larger than k^2 words, we can keep a $k \times k$ submatrix of C and calculate all elements of A which can be calculated. In this case, the operation count is $2mk^2$ and the data access is $4mk$. Thus, here the necessary memory bandwidth is $16/k$ in terms of the B/F number. If we can make $k > 200$, the necessary B/F number becomes less than 0.1, which is smaller than the actual B/F numbers of most of modern processors. The requirement of $k > 200$ means that the on-chip memory must be larger than $8 \times 200^2 = 320\,\text{kB}$, which is also satisfied for most of the modern processors. We can generalize this relation as

$$S > 2048/b^2, \tag{2.3}$$

where S is the size of the cache in bytes and b is the B/F number of the processor.

In the case of the matrix-matrix multiplication, we can apply the cache blocking at each level of the cache hierarchy. For example, if we have 64 KB of L1 cache with B/F = 4, 1 MB of L2 cache with B/F = 2, 4 MB of L3 cache with B/F = 0.5, and the main memory of B/F = 0.1. From Eq. 2.3, the necessary sizes of L1, L2, L3 caches are 64 B, 8 kB and 200 kB. Here, we ignored the effect of the cache access latency, which makes this kind of analysis far more difficult.

The above analysis can be generalized to multicore systems. Consider the case that L3 cache in the above example is shared by multiple cores, each with its own L2 cache. The matrix on L3 cache has the one-dimensional size of 160, and that on L2 32. Thus, unless we have more than 25 cores, it is easy to parallelize the cache-blocked matrix-matrix multiplication and distribute them to multiple cores, as far as each core has the cache access bandwidth equivalent to B/F number of 0.5. This is the case for all levels of the memory hierarchy.

It is certainly true that the dense matrix-matrix multiplication can make very good use of the multiple levels of cache memory. We can now ask two questions:

(a) How effective is it for other operations?
(b) Is it the the best way to handle matrix multiplication?

We will discuss these questions in more general way in later chapters, but let us briefly discuss them here.

Concerning the first question, clearly the answer depends on the characteristics of applications. If the numerical scheme used is the explicit time stepping on a regular grid, the efficient use of the hierarchical cache is difficult, since we do not have simple relationship like Eq. 2.3 for the explicit time stepping.

Very roughly, if we consider a single-stage explicit time-stepping with m variables per grid point and p operations per timestep per grid point, unless we do not use techniques like temporal blocking[4–6], the necessary bandwidth in terms of the B/F number is given by

$$b_e = \frac{16m}{p}, \tag{2.4}$$

at least in the limit of large cache size. Typically m is between five and ten for three-dimensional calculation and p is of the order of several thousands. Thus, we have $b_e \sim 0.05$ for these typical values. Since the size of the cache is finite, some of the grid points loaded to the cache memory is used only to update their neighboring grid points. If the calculation on one grid point needs the data of grid points with grid distance s, when we load the data of n^3 grid points we can only update $(n - 2s)^3$ grid points. In this case, the necessary memory bandwidth is given by

$$b_{e,n,s} = 8\frac{n^3 + (n - 2s)^3}{(n - 2s)^3 p} = 8\left[\left(\frac{1}{1 - 2s/n}\right)^3 + 1\right]/p, \tag{2.5}$$

Fig. 2.4 The relation of q
and $S' = S/(6\,\text{ms}^3)$

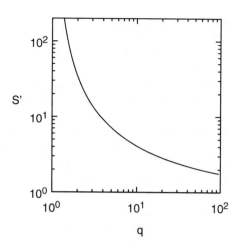

On the other hand, the relation between n and S is given by

$$S = 8mn^3, \tag{2.6}$$

and therefore we have

$$n = (S/m)^{1/3}/2. \tag{2.7}$$

Thus if we express term $2s/n$ in Eq. 2.5 as X, it is given by

$$X = 4s\left(\frac{m}{S}\right)^{1/3}. \tag{2.8}$$

If we allow the B/F number q times larger than the limiting value of Eq. 2.4, we
need

$$X < 1 - (2q - 1)^{-1/3}, \tag{2.9}$$

and thus

$$S > 64\,\text{ms}^3[1 - (2q - 1)^{-1/3}]^{-3}, \tag{2.10}$$

Figure 2.4 shows the relation between q and the normalized value of S, S',
defined as

$$S' = S/(64\,\text{ms}^3). \tag{2.11}$$

In the limit of the infinitely large cache size, we have $q = 1$. The other limit is
$q = \infty$ for $S' = 1$. Thus, both limits are clearly unpractical, and the practical

ranges of q and S' are rather narrow, like $3 < q < 20$ and $20 > S' > 3$. This behavior is quite different from the case of dense matrix-matrix multiplication, for which we can reduce the memory bandwidth by a factor of $O(1/\sqrt{S})$ as we increase the cache size S.

As in the case of the matrix-matrix multiplication, it is in principle possible to make use of the hierarchy of the cache memories. Consider the case we have L1D and L2 caches as well as LLC. If the size of L2D cache is 1/16 of that of LLC, the bandwidth between L2D and LLC must be much higher than that between the main memory and LLC. If LLC has $S' = 30$, for the main memory the necessary bandwidth is given by $q \sim 2$. On the other hand, for $S' = 2$, $q \sim 60$. This means that LLC must be 30 times faster than the main memory, which is clearly unpractical. In the case of the matrix multiplication, LLC need to be only a factor of four faster, which is not easy but not impossible. For structured-mesh calculations, hierarchical cache memories of modern microprocessors are not very useful.

2.1.7 Alternatives to Cache Memories

Concerning the second question, we consider alternative designs. One extreme example would be the design in which one processor core has only two levels of the memory hierarchy, the local memory and the global memory. This is similar to what has been adopted in CDC 7600. In the case of multicore or manycore processors, this approach has been adopted in several designs, including Sony/IBM Cell[7] and Sunway SW26010[8].

The SW26010 processor consists of four clusters, each with one management processing element (MPE) and 64 computing processing element (CPE). They have the same architecture with instruction caches, but MPE has usual data cache hierarchy and CPE has a local memory in the address space separate from that of the main memory. CPE can access the main memory through both the usual load/store instructions and DMA. In addition, 64 CPEs are organized into an 8×8 grid, and there are hardware-level support for broadcast and point-to-point operations in both directions.

With processors like SW26010, a natural way to implement the matrix-matrix multiplication

$$A = B \cdot C + D, \tag{2.12}$$

where A and D are matrices of size $m \times n$, B is that of size $m \times k$ and C $k \times n$. is to keep $k \times k$ matrix (a sub-matrix of B) distributed to local memories of CPEs and send small parts of C and D to obtain the corresponding part of A. Here, broadcast and reduction in one dimension are useful to implement matrix-matrix multiplication.

This approach of local memory and broadcast network has several advantages over the traditional approach of hierarchical cache.

- All memory cells on a processor chip can be used to store $k \times k$ matrix, resulting in the most efficient bandwidth reduction
- The power and area efficiencies of the local memories are much higher than those of L1D caches.
- data transfer through broadcast network is much cheaper compared to data sharing through hierarchical cache.

In the case of the hierarchical cache, the reduction factor of the necessary memory bandwidth to the off-chip main memory depends on the size of LLC. Here, the LLC must be shared by all cores, and a large fraction of the data loaded to LLC is used by all cores. Consider the case that we have p cores and LLC has a $k \times k$ matrix.

Figure 2.5 shows the basic matrix-matrix multiplication. We show only small parts of matrices A, B, C, D. Here, the important point is that we keep B in the on-chip memory and load small parts of C and D to obtain the corresponding part of A.

Figure 2.6 shows one way to parallelize the basic multiplication over p processors (the case of $p = 4$ is shown). Here, B is divided to four submatrices, and processor i performs $A_i = B_i \times C + D$.

In this case, the "width" of the matrices is reduced from k to k/p. On the other hand, C and D are not subdivided. Thus, each processor should receive entire C and D. In the usual architecture with hierarchical cache, this means that LLC is accessed p times, resulting in the increase of the necessary access bandwidth of LLC and also the increase in the power consumption. If there is some way to "broadcast" data to all processors, the cost of data transfer in the chip would be significantly reduced.

We can also divide B in the other direction, as shown in Fig. 2.7. In this case, A is calculated as the reduction of partial results calculated on processors as follows,

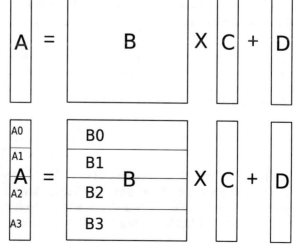

Fig. 2.5 The basic matrix-matrix operation. Here, we assume B (or a part of B has the size of $k \times k$, and is kept in the on-chip memory. Small part of C and D are loaded and $A = B \times C + D$ is performed

Fig. 2.6 The matrix-matrix operation with one-dimensional matrix division and broadcast. We show the case of $p = 4$

Fig. 2.7 The matrix-matrix operation with one-dimensional matrix division and reduction. We show the case of $p = 4$

Fig. 2.8 The matrix-matrix operation with two-dimensional matrix division. We show the case of $p = 16$

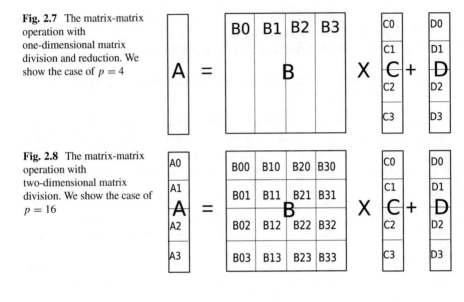

$$A = \sum_i B_i \times C_i + D_i, \tag{2.13}$$

In this case, processor i need to load only C_i and D_i, but would produce the matrix of the size same as that of A. These partial results must be summed, and that would be a rather expensive operation on machines with hierarchical cache. A naive implementation would be that each processor write its partial result, and then reduction is done using multiple processors. Here, even though the access to C and D are reduced, that for A is increased by the same amount. If there is some hardware support for the reduction of data in different processors, this additional data access can be completely removed.

It is also possible to divide B in both directions, as shown in Fig. 2.8. Here we show the case for 16 processors. Processor ij keeps submatrix B_{ij} and performs

$$A_{ij} = \sum_p B_{ij} \times C_j + D_j, \tag{2.14}$$

and the reduction is taken over i so that

$$A_j = \sum_i A_{ij}. \tag{2.15}$$

In this case, C and D are broadcasted to j direction and reduction is taken over i direction. The amount of data one processor loads or stores is reduced by a factor proportional to $\sqrt{p}$. On the other hand, with cache-based architecture the amount of data access to LLC is increased by the same factor. With hardware support for broadcast and reduction, we can avoid the increase of the data access to LLC, and that actually means there is no need for LLC.

We conclude that the necessary amount of on-chip memories and on-chip communication bandwidth to achieve the same level of performance is quite different for the traditional architecture with hierarchical cache and an alternative architecture with local memory and broadcast/reduction support, at least for the case of matrix-matrix multiplication. The reduction in the amount of data access to LLC is $O(\sqrt{p})$, where p is the number of processors which share one LLC. Using multiple levels of shared cache, we can reduce the additional bandwidth of LLC to two times that of the main memory, but we need $\log_4 p + 1$ levels of caches, each with the same amount of total memory. Thus, there will be significant increase both in the chip size and power consumption.

For the case of explicit time-stepping schemes, architecture with local memory architecture is more efficient. Since all on-chip memory area can be used for the local memory the aggregate data transfer rate of the local memory to register files and arithmetic units is very high. The B/F number of four is not difficult to achieve for local memory, but seems nearly impossible for LLC.

2.2 The Need for Quantitative Approach

In Sect. 2.1, we have seen that the direction of the evolution of processor architecture since CDC 6600 and Cray-1 is rather evolutionary or empirical than theory-driven. In the case of vector-parallel architecture, the B/F number was maintained high even after it has become difficult. As a result, the performance improvement slowed down, and distributed-memory parallel machines based on scalar microprocessors have taken over.

The history of the evolution of scalar microprocessors is not much different from that of vector-parallel machines, except that the hierarchical cache is used. As the number of cores increased, the number of the levels of cache hierarchy increased and the B/F number of the main memory slowly decreased. The efficiency of the matrix-matrix multiplication has been kept reasonably high. It is possible to reduce the B/F number while keeping the efficiency of matrix-matrix multiplication by increasing the size of LLC. The efficiency of matrix-matrix multiplication was kept high to keep high efficiency for the High-Performance Linpack benchmark (HPL), which is still used for the Top500 ranking.

On the other hand, the efficiencies of almost all other applications are not so high as that of HPL and decrease as the number of cores and the SIMD width increase. In addition, even for the case of the matrix-matrix multiplication, GPGPU chips outperform modern CPU chips both in the peak performance and the performance per watt. On the other hand, the transition from CPUs to GPGPUs have not occurred yet. GPGPUs are used for limited areas of applications, most notably the machine learning. For many other application area CPUs are still mainly used.

The fundamental problem here is that the evolution of the architecture of processors up to now is really an evolution very much like the biological evolution, without the underlying scientific principles. We talk about efficiencies and performance per watt, but we do not know how they are determined, in particular, we do not know the theoretical limit for the performance per watt. Therefore, we do not know how good a processor design is.

Many fields of engineering have underlying principle. One example is the thermal engine, for which the upper limit of the efficiency is clearly defined and determined by the first and second laws of thermodynamics. Given the temperature of the heat source T_h and that of the environment T_e, When an engine gets heat Q_h from heat source, generates work W, and emits Q_e to the environments, these quantities should satisfy

$$Q_h = W + Q_e,   \tag{2.16}$$

$$-\frac{Q_h}{T_h} + \frac{Q_e}{T_e} \geq 0.   \tag{2.17}$$

Here, Eq. 2.16 is the first law of thermodynamics, or the conservation of the energy, and inequality 2.17 is the second law of thermodynamics, or the law of the increase of the entropy. From these relations we have

$$\eta = \frac{W}{Q_h} < \eta_{\text{ideal}} = \frac{T_h - T_e}{T_e} = \frac{T_h}{T_e} - 1.   \tag{2.18}$$

Here, we define the efficiency η as W/Q_h, the ratio of the energy converted to other form (for example the electricity) to the total amount of the generated heat. Inequality 2.18 tells us that the efficiency of any engine which converts the thermal energy to other forms is lower than $T_h/T_e - 1$. Thus, in order to make η high, we should try two approaches:

- To make T_h as high as possible
- To make actual η as close to η_{ideal} as possible for given T_h

The important point here is that, once we fix T_h, the theoretical limit of the efficiency is determined, and we can measure efficiency of actual systems using this limit as the scale. As a result, we can compare different designs in terms of this efficiency relative to the theoretical limit. Of course, in many cases T_h is also determined by the design, and thus to make T_h high is equally important. For example, in the case of internal combustion engine, we can make T_h high by increasing the compression ratio, but we cannot make T_h arbitrarily high due to physical and chemical limits.

Thus, using T_h, theoretical limit of η and actual values of η, we can compare heat engines of completely different designs, such as internal combustion engines and steam and gas turbines, and also we can tell how good a design is.

Fig. 2.9 Sopwith Camel. An UK WWI fighter airplane. Author: Sanjay Acharya, This file is licensed under the Creative Commons Attribution-Share Alike 4.0 International license

Jones [9] introduced similar concept of efficiency to the design of airplanes. Here the question is what is the theoretical minimum power we need to make an airplane of given weight and wing area to fly at given speed. The answer is that the drag force on an airplane D consists of three components: induced drag, skin friction drag, and form or parasite drag. The induced drag is the drag associated with the lift force generated by a wing with a finite span. We can make the induced drag of a wing with given area smaller by making the wing span larger. The skin friction drag comes from the dissipation at the boundary layer of the airflow around the airplane, and proportional to the total surface area of the airplane. These two terms are determined by wing span, wing area and the total surface area. The last term, the form drag, is everything other than the first two terms. Thus, in order to improve the speed and reduce the necessary power, we should minimize the form drag.

Figures 2.9 and 2.10 shows two designs with very different form drag coefficients: An WWI fighter airplane Sopwith Camel, and the Spirit of Saint Louis, the first airplane to make the direct flight from New York to Paris.

Even without knowing the concept of induced, skin friction and form drags, we can see that the design of the Spirit of Saint Louis would create less drag compared to that of Sopwith Camel, with monoplane design without bracing wires. However, Jones succeeded in quantifying the difference and made clear what is the theoretical limit of the efficiency of the design of an airplane.

Fig. 2.10 The Spirit of Saint Louis. The airplane with the best design in terms of the efficiency at the time when [9] was published. Copylight: Ad Meskens, URL: https://en.wikipedia.org/wiki/Spirit_of_St._Louis#/media/File:Spirit_Of_St_Louis2.jpg, Author: Gerd Isenberg This file is licensed under the Creative Commons Attribution-ShareAlike 3.0 Unported (CC BY-SA 3.0)

2.3   What Is Measured and What Is Not

Our central question in this book is whether or not we can construct a similar measure for computer architecture. The common-sense answer would be "No". How we can compare, for example, Intel Xeon, Fujitsu A64fx, NVIDIA A100, PEZY-SC2, and Sunway SW26010 with a single measure?

The traditional approach is to come up with some set of benchmark programs. There are many such benchmarks. such as whetstone, Dhrystone, Livermore loops, SPEC CPU (int and fp, 92, 95, 2000, 2006, and 2017[10]), SLALOM[11], HPL[12], HPCC[13], HPCG[14] and more.

The fact that there are so many of them and some of them are replaced regularly means that they themselves do not represent a measure like the thermodynamical efficiency of heat engines or the form drag of airplanes.

There is one difference between the performance of computer architecture and that of heat engines or airplanes. The performance of a computer architecture cannot be measured without application programs. Some architecture would be good for some applications, while some other architecture would be good for some other applications. Both heat engines and airplane are single-purpose and do just one thing. However, a processor is multi-purpose, and calculates many different things depending on the program supplied. This is of course the reason why most of the benchmarks above consist of multiple programs (around ten in most cases).

Clearly, we do not want to measure the performance of a computer architecture with a single application. The performance of an architecture for regular grid applications can be quite different from that for particle-based applications, or that for irregular-grid applications.

Now we can ask two questions:

1. Can we define a reasonable set of applications for which we want to measure the efficiency of an architecture?
2. For a given application, how we can actually measure and compare the efficiency of different architectures?

In the next chapter, we will address these two questions.

References

1. J.E. Thornton, *Design of a Computer the Control Data 6600* (Scott, Foresman and Company, Glenvew, 1970)
2. J.S. Kolodzey, IEEE Trans. Components Hybrids Manuf. Technol. **4**(2), 181 (1981)
3. J. Hennessy, D. Patterson, *Computer Architecture: A Quantitative Approach* (Morgan Kaufmann, San Francisco, 1990)
4. M. Wolfe, in *Proceedings Supercomputing '89* (IEEE, Los Alamitos, 1989), pp. 655–664
5. J. Ragan-Kelley, C. Barnes, A. Adams, S. Paris, F. Durand, S. Amarasinghe, ACM SIGPLAN Notices **48**(6), 519 (2013)
6. T. Muranushi, J. Makino, Proc. Comput. Sci. **51**, 1303 (2015)
7. A. Arevalo, R.M. Matinata, M. Pandian, E. Peri, K. Ruby, F. Thomas, C. Almond, Programming the cell broadband engine^{TM} architecture examples and best practices (2008). http://www.redbooks.ibm.com/redbooks/pdfs/sg247575.pdf
8. H. Fu, J. Liao, J. Yang, L. Wang, Z. Song, X. Huang, C. Yang, W. Xue, F. Liu, F. Qiao, W. Zhao, X. Yin, C. Hou, C. Zhang, W. Ge, J. Zhang, Y. Wang, C. Zhou, G. Yang, Sci. China Infor. Sci. **59**(7), 072001 (2016). https://doi.org/10.1007/s11432-016-5588-7
9. B. Melvill Jones, J. R. Aeronaut. Soc. **33**(221), 357–385 (1929). https://doi.org/10.1017/S0368393100136442
10. J. Bucek, K.D. Lange, J. v. Kistowski, in *Companion of the 2018 ACM/SPEC International Conference on Performance Engineering, ICPE '18* (Association for Computing Machinery, New York, 2018), pp. 41–42. https://doi.org/10.1145/3185768.3185771
11. J. Gustafson, D. Rover, S. Elbert, M. Carter, Supercomput. Rev. **3**(11), 56 (1990)
12. J.J. Dongarra, P. Luszczek, A. Petitet, Concurrency Comput. Pract. Experience **15**(9), 803 (2003). https://doi.org/10.1002/cpe.728. https://onlinelibrary.wiley.com/doi/abs/10.1002/cpe.728
13. P.R. Luszczek, D.H. Bailey, J.J. Dongarra, J. Kepner, R.F. Lucas, R. Rabenseifner, D. Takahashi, in *Proceedings of the 2006 ACM/IEEE Conference on Supercomputing* (Citeseer, 2006), pp. 1188455–1188677
14. J.J. Dongarra, A. Heroux, Michael, P. Luszczek, Hpcg benchmark:a new metric for ranking high performance computing systems. Tech. Rep. 15-736, Department of Electrical Engineering and Computer Science, University of Tennessee System (2015). http://www.eecs.utk.edu/resources/library/594

Chapter 3
The Lower Limit of Energy Consumption

You can't win, you can't break even, and you can't get out of the game.

— Allen Ginsberg

3.1 Range of Applications We Consider

We ended the previous chapter with the following two questions.

1. Can we define a reasonable set of applications for which we want to measure the efficiency of an architecture?
2. For a given application, how we can actually measure and compare the efficiency of different architectures?

We discuss the first question in this section. One possibility is to look at benchmark programs used for recent supercomputer projects. One such example is Fugaku project (formerly know as post-K). It adopted nine "target applications"[1] shown in Table 3.1.

EuroEXA project[2] lists 15 applications in Table 3.2. They stress the following four measures:

- FLOPS
- IOPS
- Memory bandwidth
- Memory capacity

US Exascale project[3] lists the 20 applications in Table 3.3.

Most of these applications perform time-marching simulations, and some of the rest perform iterative optimizations. All applications deal with systems with a large

---

[1] https://postk-web.r-ccs.riken.jp/appl.html.

[2] https://euroexa.eu/.

[3] https://www.exascaleproject.org/research-group/.

© Springer Nature Switzerland AG 2021
J. Makino, *Principles of High-Performance Processor Design*,
https://doi.org/10.1007/978-3-030-76871-3_3

Table 3.1 Target applications of Fugaku project

Applications	Description
GENESIS	MD for proteins
Genomon	Genome processing (Genome alignment)
GAMERA	Earthquake simulator (FEM in unstructured and structured grid)
NICAM+LETKF	Weather prediction system using Big data (structured grid stencil and ensemble Kalman filter)
NTChem	Molecular electronic (structure calculation)
Adventure	Computational Mechanics System for Large Scale Analysis and Design (unstructured grid)
RSDFT	An ab-initio program (density functional theory)
FFB	Large Eddy Simulation (unstructured grid)
LQCD	Lattice QCD simulation (structured grid Monte Carlo)

Table 3.2 Co-design applications of EuroEXA project

Applications	Description
AVU-GSR	Gaia data reconstruction
Quantum Espresso	DFT (Density Functional Theory)
SMURFF	Scalable Matrix Factorization Framework
Neuromarketing	?
NEMO	Ocean model
Astronomy image classification	?
NEST/DPSNN	Brain simulation
FRTM	Seismic analyses, finite difference
InfOli	biological-neuron simulator
IFS	ECMWF's weather forecast model. Spectral method
LBM	Lattice Boltzmann methods
Alya	Multiphysics simulation code for engineering applications. Irregular mesh.
Gadget	Cosmological Nbody+hydro code. Particles
LFRic	Weather and Climate, Cubed-sphere, semi-implicit

degree of freedom using parallel computation. We classify the parallel computation on systems with large degree of freedoms into the following categories

(a) Regular/structured mesh
(b) Unstructured mesh
(c) Particles
(d) "Random" Graphs
(e) Dense matrices

We first briefly discuss the characteristics of each category.

Table 3.3 Co-design applications of US Exascale project

Applications	Description
LatticeQCD	Lattice QCD simulation (structured grid Monte Carlo)
NWChemEx	Quantum Chemistry
GAMESS	Quantum Chemistry
EXAALT	Molecular Dynamics
ExaAM	Simulator for Additive Manufacturing
QMCPACK	Material design with Quantum Monte Carlo
ExaStar	Supernova
ExaSky	Cosmological N-body (+Hydro)
EQSIM	seismic wave propagation model
Subsurface	multiphysics CFD for reservoir simulation
E3SM-MMF	Local climate model
ExaWind	CFD for wind plant
Combustion-PELE	Combustion engine model
MFIX-Exa	CFD-DEM
WDMApp	ITER simulator
ExaSMR	Simulator for Small Modular Reactors
WarpX	Modeling Particle Accelerators, PIC with AMR
Ristra	Multi-physics simulation tools for weapons-relevant applications, irregular mesh
MAPP	Multi-physics simulation tools for High Energy Density Physics, ALE, finite difference
EMPIRE AND SPARC	electromagnetic plasma physics, reentry aerodynamics

3.1.1 Structured Mesh

Structured mesh means that the computational degree of freedoms is expressed as multidimensional arrays which can be nested to express adaptive resolutions. This structure usually appears when we discretize the two or three-dimensional space with the finite-difference or finite-volume method. In three dimensions, a grid point is specified by three indices, for example i, j, and k, and in the simplest case they correspond to three components of the coordinate directly. It is possible to map, for example, a rectangular mesh to curved coordinates around an airfoil, or to map a cube to a sphere, to express shapes which are not a simple rectangle or rectangular solid. NICAM, LQCD, NEMO, FRTM, IFS, LBM, LFRic, LatticeQCD, ExaAM, ExaStar, EQSIM, E3SM-MMF, WarpX, and MAPP fall to this category.

From the computational point of view, applications in this category are relatively easy to parallelize on large-scale HPC systems, since the optimal way to distribute the computation is to divide the grid to small sub-grids and assign each of them to one computational process. The communication between processes are usually limited to neighbors, though there are cases where some global communications are required. In some cases, the Poisson equation need to be solved, and the fast and accurate way to solve the Poisson equation on the structured mesh is FFT. The performance of FFT on massively parallel system is limited by the bisection bandwidth [1], but this is rather exceptional.

On the node level, the performance of applications of this structured mesh category is usually limited by the memory bandwidth. The memory access pattern is usually contiguous and thus the near-peak performance is achieved for the memory access.

3.1.2   Unstructured Mesh

Many applications in engineering need to deal with complex shapes which are not easily mapped to structured mesh. Thus, unstructured mesh is used in many engineering applications. Finite-Element Method (FEM) is usually used to discretize the space, and this means we need to solve a sparse and unstructured matrix iteratively. Once an unstructured mesh is generated, mesh points are numbered, and in the case of FEM the elements (either tetrahedron or hexahedron in three dimensions or triangle or quadrilateral in two dimensions) are also numbered, and we generate the mapping table between grid points and elements. Mathematically, FEM starts from equations for each element and constructs overall system of equations from element equations. Thus, mesh points and their physical quantities are accessed through mapping tables between elements and mesh points. This means that the memory access is not contiguous but indirect. Moreover, the global equation is solved iteratively, in many cases using preconditioned CG (conjugate-gradient) method. This means that the number of floating-point operations performed per memory access is small. The HPCG benchmark is designed to mimic this behavior of unstructured mesh applications, and the required B/F number of HPCG benchmark is around six [2]. Thus, the efficiency of modern supercomputers measured by the HPCG benchmark is very low, between 1 and 3 percentiles, except for NEC SX-ACE (the successor of SX-9) which can still get around 10% [2]. The efficiency of SX-Aurora went down to around 6%.

GAMERA, Adventure, FFB, SMURFF, Alya, Subsurface, ExaWind, Combustion-PELE, MFIX-Exa, WDMApp, ExaSMR, Ristra, EMPIRE AND SPARC probably fall to this category. Some of them do not provide sufficient information.

3.1.3   Particles

When we model materials at the molecular level, or model biological molecules, the basic tool is the classical molecular dynamics in which molecules are expressed as atoms interacting through simple classical forces. Thus, we have systems of atoms interacting through bonds, non-bonding van der Waals forces, and electrostatic forces. When we model galaxies as collection of stars interact through gravity, we also have a system of interacting particles. We can also model fluids, solids, or complex mixture of them as corrections of particles, through many different ways of discretization. Particle-based methods can be used for complex geometries as unstructured mesh can, but most of particle-based method do not require iterations to solve the overall equation. In addition, the number of particles one particle interact in one timestep is generally large, between several hundreds and tens of thousands. This means that the particle-based calculations are generally more expensive compared to unstructured mesh calculations, but at the same time that the required B/F is rather small and the efficiency can be fairly high. Efficiencies higher than 30% have been reported [3, 4].

GENESIS, Gadget, EXAALT, and ExaSky fall to this category.

3.1.4 Random Graphs

Both of structured and unstructured meshes are essentially the discretization of an continuum. "Random" graphs are of different origin. good examples are simulators for large digital circuits, such as a microprocessor. NEST/DPSNN and InfOli might fall to this category.

3.1.5 Dense Matrices

Simulation based on Quantum Mechanics requires the diagonalization of large dense matrices, and thus for many applications in material science and biochemistry, the operations on Dense matrices is the most expensive part.

NTChem, Quantum Espresso, NWChemEx, GAMMES, and QMCPACK fall to this category. Though not included in any of exascale project, deep learning applications also fall to this category.

3.1.6 Miscellanies

We cannot classify Astronomy image classification and AVU-GSR since not much details are available.

GENOMON [5] is a suite of bioinformatics tools for analyzing cancer genome and RNA sequencing data. Its core is bwa-mem [6], which uses the Burrows-Wheeler transform [7] to align short-reads from DNA sequencers with the reference genome. Its algorithm is pointer-chasing and could be classified to random graph category.

Table 3.4 Number of
applications in each category

Type	Count
Structured mesh	14
Unstructured mesh	13
Particles	4
Random Graphs	2
Dense Matrices	3
Miscellanies	3

Table 3.4 Number of applications in each category

3.1.7 Distribution of Application Types

Table 3.4 shows, for each category, the number of applications selected for three exascale projects. We can see that the categories we introduced are reasonable in the sense that most of applications can be categorized. Around 1/3 of all applications fall to the category of structured mesh, and another 1/3 to unstructured mesh. Particles, Dense Matrices and Random Graphs share the rest.

Of course, the number of applications does not directly indicate the importance of the method. Our observation here is that our five categories do cover the majority of HPC applications.

As I wrote above, deep learning applications falls to the Dense Matrices category, and thus the importance of this category is currently large and increasing. Many of the algorithms to analyze "big data" falls to Random Graphs category. However, in many cases the analysis part is more like particle-based simulations. For example, many clustering algorithms are based on the movement of data points using the interaction between them defined to achieve clustering. Many of other classical data analysis methods are based on dense matrix diagonalization. Thus, we believe many of the expensive calculations in data science are categorized to particle based or dense matrices.

3.2 Definition of Efficiency

Now we have a fairly limited number of categories of applications. It should be possible to define efficiencies for each category.

The first question is what should be maximized when we design the processor architecture for a specific category of applications. In the case of thermal engine, what we want to maximize is the efficiency of conversion from thermal energy to other forms of energy, and the theoretical limit is given by the second law of the thermodynamics. In the case of airplane design, what should be minimized is the form drag, where zero is the theoretical limit.

It seems natural to define the efficiency of a processor architecture for a specific application (or a category of applications) as the ratio of the minimum amount of energy required to complete one calculation for that application and actual amount of energy consumed. Let us investigate if we can use this definition.

One obvious problem is that the amount of energy depends on the semiconductor technology used. With a more advanced semiconductor technology, the power consumption of a same processor design can be reduced. For nearly a half century, semiconductor technology has been advancing following Moore's law. The exponential advance following Moore's law is clearly one reason why the comparison of different processor designs have been difficult. How we can compare, for example, a processor made with Intel's "0.6 μm" process with Fujitsu's "0.6 μm" process? Even for the processors from the same company, how we can compare a design for "0.6 μm" process with that for "14 nm" process?

Fortunately for the comparison purpose but unfortunately for the computer industry, the advance of the semiconductor technology following Moore's law is approaching to its end, as we discussed in Sect. 2.1.4. First, the reduction of the supply voltage and the increase of the clock speed both ended with the 90 nm process. Then the reduction in the parasite capacitance, which determines the power consumption of CMOS device, slowed down when we move from planar (or so-called bulk-CMOS) device to three-dimensional FinFET device. At the same time, shrink in the size of the transistor has become slow, and the cost of the LSI device per transistor started to increase. These changes, in particular the *increase* of the transistor cost, really mean we are seeing the end of the exponential advance of the semiconductor technology we have enjoyed for the last half century, and it is the essential reason why we should reconsider the way we design processor architectures. If the advance of the semiconductor technology really has reached an end, we should have one single "best" fabrication process with which any processor should be designed, and thus the problem of comparing the processors designed and made with different semiconductor technology automatically vanishes. Though we have not yet reached that point, we are not very far from it.

Thus, at least in principle, we will be able to compare different processors, even when they are made using different device technology, because the difference between different technologies will become small. On the other hand, in practice, there will remain the differences, since there will remain the choice for the transistor size and driving capacity, as well as the core supply voltage, even when we chose one semiconductor technology. In other words, we should be able to define the "best possible processor architecture" for a given semiconductor technology, a give supply voltage, and a given application.

The "best" architecture should be defined as minimizing some quantity. If we take the analogy of heat engines and airplanes, the energy we need to perform the same operation for a given application would be a natural choice.

In the past, the cost of the electricity had not been the dominant term of the total cost of HPC systems. This is because the lifetime of a machine had been relatively short. Typical replacement cycle of an HPC center had been 4 or 5 years. The replacement cycle had been short because of the exponential improvement of the performance. Let us assume that we have the budget for buy/lease computers for the next 10 years. If we know that in 5 years we will be able to buy a computer ten times faster than what is available now, it would make sense to keep half of the total budget for the that machine and use the other half to buy a computer now. For the first 5 years, we will operate what is available now. After 5 years, we will buy a new machine which is ten times faster, for the same price and similar power consumption. At this moment, it would not make sense to operate the old one, since keeping the old computer would add only 10% of performance, for twice the space and electricity. Thus, the lifetime of a computer is essentially the development cycle of new generations. If we can buy four times faster machine in every 3 years, essentially the same argument would be valid. Thus, while the exponential increase of the performance of computers was continuing, the lifetime of computers were short. However, as we have already seen, the exponential increase, at least in the side of the semiconductor technology, is now close to its end. As a result, the lifetime of computers will be longer, and that means the electricity cost will eventually dominate the total cost.

Moreover, The power consumption of high-end microprocessors have increased drastically in the last three decades. In 1990, microprocessors used in commercial workstations were either Motorola 68030 or RISC chips such as MIPS R3000 or Sun SPARC. The power consumption of these chips were 5–10 W. Personal computers were equipped with Intel 486DX. The power consumption of these chips were also 5–10 W.

In 1992, DEC Alpha 21064 (at 200 MHz clock) consumed around 30 W, and in 1997 Pentium II (at 233 MHz clock) consumed 35 W. In 1999, DEC Alpha 21264 (at 600 MHz clock) consumed 73 W. Thus, we can see that the power consumption of microprocessors had increased by nearly a factor of 10 in 1990s. In 2004, Intel Pentium 4 2.4 GHz reached the power consumption of 115 W. After this point, the increase of power consumption continued, but with a much slower pace. As of 2020, AMD Ryzen Threadripper 3990X consumes 280 W, and Intel Xeon W-3175X consumes 255 W.

When these modern processors are used for HPC systems, the electricity cost would become comparable to the hardware cost. The cost of electricity is 0.1–0.2 USD/kWh, depending on countries. If we take the number of 0.2, The electricity cost of a processor with 300 W power consumption would be 530 USD/year. Of course, the actual cost would be somewhat higher since the total power consumption is larger due to the loss in the power supply and power consumption of other units like DRAM modules. On the other hand, the price of these processor is around 3000 USD. Thus, if we use these processors for 5 years, the electricity cost would be comparable or higher than the hardware cost.

Since the lifetime of processors will be longer in the future, it is quite likely that the electricity cost will be the dominant part of the total cost. We conclude that what we should minimize is the amount of the energy we need to perform a given calculation.

In practice, we should still consider other factors like the hardware cost. This is also the case for thermal engines or airplanes. Even if an engine can achieve the efficiency very close to the theoretical limit, if it is too expensive or too large for the given power, it is of no practical use. We of course apply similar practical considerations to our processor architecture. Important observation here is that we should define a quantitative measure of the efficiency of a computer processor design as its energy consumption relative to the theoretical minimum energy for a given semiconductor technology, a given supply voltage, and a given application.

We should now define the minimum energy for a given semiconductor technology, a give supply voltage, and a given application. Here, we try the approach similar to that used for airplanes. In the case of airplanes, the aerodynamic drag force is classified to three categories: induced drag, surface friction drag and form drag. The first two terms cannot be reduced, if we specify the wing span and wing area. Thus, the remaining term, the form drag, directly indicates the loss of the efficiency. The point here is that we should be able to classify the power consumption to the reducible and irreducible terms.

When we run the HPC applications, in almost all cases we do intensive floating-point operations, based on some numerical scheme. When we specify the numerical scheme used, for a given problem there should be a minimum necessary number for the required floating-point operations, N_{min}. For a given semiconductor technology and a given supply voltage, there must be a design of the floating-point arithmetic logic circuit which gives the minimum energy consumption, p_{min} (in J). Now for a given semiconductor technology, a given supply voltage, and a given application, the minimum energy consumption is given by

$$P_{min} = N_{min} p_{min}. \qquad (3.1)$$

We can now formally define the efficiency of a processor architecture as

$$\eta = \frac{P_{min}}{P_{actual}}, \qquad (3.2)$$

where P_{actual} is the actual energy consumed by that processor. Clearly P_{actual} is a measurable quantity, but P_{min} is difficult to estimate. One way to obtain an estimate is to isolate the power consumption of the combinatorial part of the floating-point arithmetic circuit, when it is performing useful operations, and then regard that as P_{min}. One practical advantage of this approach is that this can be easily done in simulation and thus easily used as the practical guidance of the processor design.

If it is possible to apply different numerical accuracies to different operations within an application, the above definition of P_{min} should be extended to take into account of that fact, as

$$P_{min} = \sum_{i=1}^{n} N_{min,i} p_{min,i}. \qquad (3.3)$$

Here, i is the index of the number format used, n is the number of the number format, and $N_{min,i}$ and $p_{min,i}$ are the number and power consumption of operations in that format.

Our concept of efficiency of a processor is to regard everything other than the combinatorial logic for arithmetic circuit as "form drag" of an Aeroplane. One might think that this is unpractical since on modern processors moving the data between processor and memory is the essential part of the calculation, and the circuit and power spent for the memory access cannot be regarded as useless.

In the rest of this chapter, we discuss the question: "Is it appropriate to regard everything other than the combinatorial logic for arithmetic circuit as useless waste?" We will review applications of five types in turn.

3.3 Structured Mesh

3.3.1 Choice of the Numerical Methods

As we have seen in Sect. 3.1, structured meshes are used in a large number of applications in science and engineering. Exascale applications in climate models. seismic models, Lattice-QCD calculations are typical applications. With the notable exception of the Lattice-QCD calculation where Monte-Carlo sampling is performed, most applications in which structured meshes are used solve the hyperbolic partial differential equations using the finite-difference method. Strictly speaking, the mathematical scheme could be the finite volume or other method, but from numerical point of view these scheme can be regarded as a finite-difference scheme in the sense that the value of a grid point at the new timestep is calculated from the values of a finite set of neighboring grid points in the old timestep. This means that the scheme we consider is explicit and compact.

We can list many numerical schemes which is not explicit or not compact. For example, the compact finite-difference scheme [8] is compact but not explicit. We can regard any spectral method as explicit but not compact. These schemes have computational characteristic completely different from that of explicit and compact schemes. Moreover, for many problems in CFD, including climate models, the incompressible approximation has been, and still is, used.

Thus, one might think if we limit our analysis only to explicit compact schemes, that would not cover good and practical numerical schemes.

In this section, we discuss the explicit and compact schemes only because of the following two reasons.

The first reason is that we will anyway discuss implicit schemes in relation to unstructured meshes in the next section. The requirement for the architecture is not very different.

The second reason is that recent developments of calculation schemes favor the explicit compact schemes over traditional approaches. One example is the reduced sound speed technique (RSST) [9, 10]. The basic idea of RSST is to approximate a subsonic flow with the same subsonic flow with a higher Mach number. We can intuitively see this approximation is valid from the following consideration.

For a wide range of subsonic flows, we can apply the incompressible approximation. The idea of incompressible approximation is that for many subsonic flows we can obtain an approximate solution by assuming that the speed of sound is infinite (that the fluid is incompressible). This means that flows with different Mach numbers can be approximated by a single incompressible flow, and thus flows with different Mach numbers can be regarded as approximations of each other. Consider the case where we simulate a flow with the Mach number of 0.01. If we use the explicit method, the timestep is limited by the sound speed and thus very small. If we use the incompressible approximation, we can use the timestep determined by the speed of the actual flow, and thus not limited by the sound speed. With RSST, we can, for example, simulate this flow as the flow with the Mach number of 0.1, or even 0.5, and thus use the timestep only a factor of two shorter than that for the incompressible approximation.

If the actual stepsize is different only by a factor of two, the explicit and compact schemes are likely to be faster, in particular when the resolution is high, since the per-grid calculation cost of explicit and compact schemes are independent of the problem size. With the incompressible approximation, we have to solve the Poisson equation. In three dimensions, the most widely used methods for solving the Poisson equation on regular or near-regular grids are FFT or Multigrid iteration. The calculation cost of FFT has the $O(\log N)$ term, where N is the total number of the grid points. In addition, on parallel computers with distributed-memory architecture, the performance of parallel FFT is limited by the bisection bandwidth of the network [11–13], and thus not likely to increase as fast as the speed of computation. In fact, the measured performance of very well optimized FFT code on 8192 nodes of K computer (theoretical peak speed of 1.05 Pflops) is 18 Tflops, less than 2% of the peak performance [14]. K computer had six-dimensional torus network and thus its bisection bandwidth was exceptionally high compared to other machines with different network topology. We can see that the efficiency of FFT on modern large-scale HPC platforms is very low.

To give some idea of the relative advantage of the explicit scheme over traditional method, consider the case of spectral method with FFT. If we use FFT for 8192^3 grid, the number of floating-point operations per step per grid is around 6000 [15]. As stated above, even on K computer the efficiency of FFT is around 2%. If we do the same calculation on Fugaku, which has roughly 25 times faster CPU and two times faster network. the efficiency will be around 0.2%. On the other hand, explicit schemes can achieve the efficiency of 10–20%. Thus, the difference of the efficiency is around a factor of 100. It is certainly true that FFT would provide better resolution for the same number of the grid point. However, the difference in the speed of two orders of magnitudes is large enough to make the explicit method more useful.

3.3.2   The Design of An Ideal Processor Architecture for Structured Mesh Calculations

As we decided to limit the analysis only to explicit and compact scheme, the remaining question is whether or not it is reasonable to regard the power consumption of the combinatorial part of the floating-point arithmetic unit as the "necessary" part and everything else unnecessary. The typical number of floating-point operations per grid point per timestep is $2 \sim 4 \times 10^3$ [16], while the number of variables is five (three for velocities, one for density and one for energy or some other thermodynamical quantity). Thus, if we construct a pipelined processor which reads and writes the grid data only once per timestep, the number of memory access is around 1/1000 of the number of floating-point operations. Here, a pipelined processor will perform all operations necessary to update one grid point in a deep algorithm-specific pipeline, and thus there will be no overhead of register file access or cache memory access. Strictly speaking, small memories for neighboring grid points will be necessary, but they are small and can be integrated into the pipeline. Thus, the access cost of these memories will be practically negligible.

In addition, it is theoretically possible to reduce the amount of memory access further by temporal blocking [17–19], and actual improvement on non-trivial problem have been reported [16]. We conclude that it is reasonable to assume that when we design an ideal pipelined processor for the structured grid calculation, its power consumption will be dominated by that of the combinatorial logic circuit for the arithmetic units. In other words, we can justify our choice of taking into account only the combinatorial logic circuit for the arithmetic units when we estimate the lower limit for the power consumption.

3.4   Unstructured Mesh

The unstructured mesh is used primarily with the finite element method (FEM). The basic idea of FEM is to rewrite a partial differential equation to a variational problem (weak formulation). For the full mathematical basis see standard textbooks, e.g., [20]. Here we give the basic idea. Consider the Dirichlet boundary problem of the Poisson equation

$$-\nabla^2 u = f \quad \text{in} \quad \Omega, \tag{3.4}$$

$$u = 0 \quad \text{on} \quad \partial\Omega, \tag{3.5}$$

where $\Omega \subset \mathbb{R}^3$ is a domain (open connected set) and $\partial\Omega$ is the boundary of Ω. We define the inner product (L^2 product) of two functions u and v in Ω as

$$(u, v) = \int_\Omega uv dx. \tag{3.6}$$

By taking the inner product with v of the both side of Eq. (3.4) we have

$$-\int_{\Omega} (\nabla^2 u)v\,dx = \int_{\Omega} fv\,dx. \tag{3.7}$$

Using Green's identity and the condition that $v = 0$ on Ω, we have

$$(\nabla u, \nabla v) = (f, v). \tag{3.8}$$

Both sides of the weak form 3.8 is integral. If we discretize functions in Ω with linear combinations of a finite number of basis functions, in such a way that we can define the integral of u and ∇u, the weak form is approximated by a set of linear equations. Thus, the original Poisson equation is discretized by a set of linear equation.

If we take the basis set as, for example, the Fourier series, this method goes back to the standard way to solve the periodic boundary problem of the Poisson equation. In FEM, the basis set is constructed from finite elements. Figure 3.1 shows the example of triangle elements in two dimensions. The discretized function is constructed on each element, so that they are continuous on the boundaries between elements. In the simplest case, the number of basis functions is equal to the number of interior grid points, and for each of these grid point we have one equation derived from Eq. (3.8).

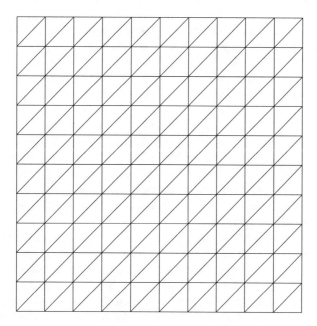

Fig. 3.1 An example of triangle elements filling a square

The advantage of FEM over the finite-difference method is that, since the weak form is based on the integration and not the differentiation, we can use elements of any shape as far as they uniquely cover Ω. Thus, domain of complex shape can be solved. In addition, the boundary condition is naturally satisfied. Thus, for many problems in engineering, FEM is the preferred method. The resulted linear system can be expressed as

$$Au = b, \tag{3.9}$$

where A is an irregular sparse matrix. The standard way to solve Eq. (3.9) is to use some sort of iterative method, since for sparse matrix the direct method such as the Gaussian elimination would be too costly both in the amount of calculation and amount of memory, except for the case of the one-dimensional problems. Multigrid methods [21] or preconditioned conjugate gradient (CG) method [22, 23] are usually used.

Though both methods apply some transformations to matrix A, in both cases, the dominant operation is the matrix-vector multiplication of the form of $A'u$ with matrix A' derived from the original matrix A, and the preconditioner is usually carefully designed so that the number of non-zero elements of A' is not significantly larger than that of A. Thus, as far as the nature of the calculation is concerned, we can regard the dominant part of any FEM calculation as the matrix-vector operation but with very sparse matrix. For example, when the three-dimensional hexahedral element is used. the number of non-zero elements per one row of A (and thus that of A') is 27.

In the usual approach, we construct A (sometimes called the global matrix) and calculate Au. If we have only one variable per grid point, we do one multiplication and one addition per one load operation of the element of A. Thus, the required memory bandwidth in terms of the B/F number is four. This value was okay for the vector-parallel machines in 1980s and 1990s, as we have seen in Chap. 2. However, modern HPC platforms have much smaller B/F numbers, and thus the achieved efficiency of FEM codes are generally very low, around a few percents. The HPCG benchmark [24] is designed to model this behavior of the CG iteration of typical FEM codes. The efficiency numbers in the June 2020 [25] are between 0.4% and 10%, with the highest score, 10%, achieved by NEC SX-ACE processor which has B/F of around 1.0. The lowest score, 0.4%, is for Sunway TaihuLight which has the B/F number of around 0.03. We can see that the efficiency of HPCG is roughly proportional to the B/F number.

Thus, one might think this is a clear example of application for which the cost of the memory access cannot be ignored. Of course, there are many approaches which effectively reduce the memory access. One example is the domain decomposition method (DDM) based on local direct solvers, or Schur complement method [26]. The DDM was originally developed to be used on distributed-memory parallel computers. The basic idea of DDM is to divide computational domain into subdomains, and "solve" the equations for the interior points of each subdomain so that we have only the equations for the values on boundaries of subdmains, which is called the interface equations. Then the interface equation is solved either iteratively or using the direct solver. Intuitively, we can eliminate the equations for the interior points, since what we solve is essentially a linear Poisson equation. Once we specify the values at boundary points of a subdomain, the values of all interior points are determined. This means that we can eliminate the interior points from the matrix equation, since they are all linearly dependent on the values of the boundary points.

For the elimination of the interior points the direct solver is used. Thus, this part is relatively computationally expensive and yet the amount of the memory access is small. On the other hand, the calculation cost of the direct elimination is pretty large. If we have n interior points and m boundary points, the calculation cost of the direct elimination is $O(nm^2)$. In three dimensions $m \propto n^{2/3}$. So the calculation cost is $O(n^{7/3})$. This can be much higher than the calculation cost of the preconditioned CG method.

Another method to reduce the memory access is the use of the element-by-element method [27, 28]. The basic idea of the element-by-element (EBE) method is to avoid the construction of the global matrix A and process each element separately. Very roughly speaking, in this way we need to read the information of each point only once per iteration, while the global matrix has the size of around $30N$, where N is the total number of points. The minimum number of data per point is four in three dimensions. (position and the value of a physical variable). Thus, we can reduce the memory access from around 30 to 4.

Yet another approach is to combine structured and unstructured meshes. The main advantage of FEM is that it can be used for objects with complex shapes. In other words, it is important that we can use elements of arbitrary shapes for region near the surface of objects. On the other hand, for the bulk of the object there is no reason to use the elements of arbitrary shapes, and thus we could use structured meshes. As far as we know that the structured mesh is used, we do not need to read the matrix elements since they can be generated with small calculation cost, and thus we need to load only the elements of u. Thus, the memory access per element is now reduced from 30 to 2 (one read and one write).

These methods (except for DDM with the direct solver for interior points) can reduce the amount of the memory access by a fair amount, like a factor of ten, but not by a factor of 100. Thus, even with these techniques, the cost of the memory access will remain to be the dominant part of FEM calculations on modern HPC platforms.

We have observed that, as far as the data are in the external DRAM and they need to be accessed for each iteration, the data access cost will be the dominant part of the total calculation cost. In other words, if we can fit the data to the on-chip memory of the processor chip, we could reduce the memory access cost by a large factor.

According to a news article [29], the SRAM cell size for TSMC 28 nm process is $0.127\,\mu m^2$. Therefore, we can fit 8M bits of memory in one mm^2 area of a chip. We need other circuits and the actual density would be more like $4\,Mbits/mm^2$. The memory of one gigabits would need $250\,mm^2$. With more advanced TSMC N5 technology, the cell size is reduced by a factor of six [30], for around $40\,mm^2$ per one gigabits.

The price of DDR4 DRAM chips (as of 2019–2020) is around 3 USD/GB. On the other hand, a 40 mm^2 chip fabricated with TSMC N5 technology would cost somewhere between 10 and 30 USD. Thus, one GB of on-chip memory would cost 80–240 USD, 30–100 times higher than the cost of DRAM chips. At first sight, it might look unpractical to even think of using on-chip memory as the primary memory. However, there are two factors we should take into account.

The first one is that the actual cost of DRAM chips for HPC systems is much higher than that of DDR4 DRAM chips. Many recent HPC system rely on HBM (High-Bandwidth Memory), a combination of three-dimensional integration of multiple DRAM chips and so-called "2.5D" integration, which means an HBM module and the processor chip are both mounted on a common silicon interposer and connected with thousands of fine patterns formed in the interposer. This technology is very expensive, and will remain to be so. The first commercial product with HBM memory is AMD Radeon R9 Fury GPU shipped in 2015. Even in 2021, HBM is used in only a handful of very high-end products, and much cheaper GDDRx memory are used for most of other products which require high memory bandwidth. A good examples are NVIDIA A100 GPGPU and GeForce RTX3090 GPU. The former has 40 GB of HBM2 memory with the total memory bandwidth of 1.6 TB/s, while the latter has 24 GB of GDDR memory with the total memory bandwidth of 936 GB/s.

Thus the actual price difference between on-chip memory and high-performance DRAM is not a factor of 100 but more like less than a factor of ten.

Another factor is that the amount of memory many unstructured-mesh calculations need is much smaller compared to the requirement of structured-mesh calculations. This is simply because of the fact that unstructured-mesh calculations typically need many iterations and thus computationally expensive. The degree of freedom for very large FEM calculations on exascale platforms would be around 10^{12}, and the size of the typical problems would be much smaller. If we assume that we need 100bytes per one grid point, 100 TB of memory would enough for exascale systems. We could put a 10TF processor to around 100 mm^2 using TSMC N5 technology. Exascale thus would need 10^7 mm^2. With the same 10^7 mm^2, we can fit 2.5×10^{14} bits, or 60 TB of memory, which is about what we need to store the data for exascale-class FEM calculations. Thus, we can see that it is not completely unpractical to use on-chip memory as the primary storage.

The total number of processor chips will be around 20 k, if we assume the chip size close to, but smaller than, 1000 mm^2. This means we have about 400^3 grid points on one chip. We do need relatively fast communication between processors. However, compared to the required memory bandwidth for the global matrix, with this grid size, the necessary network bandwidth is smaller by three orders of magnitude. The number of grid points to be communicated is proportional to the surface area of the local mesh, and thus $6/400 \sim 1/60$ of the total number of the grid points. In addition, we do not need to communicate the matrix elements and only the updated value of the grid points. In the case of simple problems with similar nature as that of HPCG, the global matrix has 27 non-zero elements per row. Thus, there is another factor of 27, and the necessary amount of communication between nodes is smaller than the memory access by a factor of $60 \times 27 = 1620$. Since the necessary B/F for the memory is 4, we need the network B/F of 0.002. If we can construct a processor with the peak floating-point performance of 100TF, the necessary network throughput of one processor is 200 GB/s. This is fairly high but not impossible for a processor with 100TF peak speed, and the power consumption of the network interface would be smaller than that of the arithmetic units.

It should be noted that just to replace the external DRAM chips by on-chip memory blocks is not enough to reduce the power consumption. In the case of HBM, the length of the pattern between the logic chip of HBM and the processor chip is comparable to or even shorter than the distance between the processor core and the DRAM interface of the processor chip. Thus, very roughly speaking, the power consumption can be similar. The actual physical connection would be quite different, since the connection between HBM logic chip and processor chip is a single wire, while the connection between the processor core and DRAM interface probably consists of hundreds of driver gates and pipeline flip-flops. The amount of energy necessary to drive one signal pattern is determined by the product of the length of the wire and its capacitance per unit length [31]. If we scale the width, height, and the distance from the ground plane of a signal pattern all by a same factor, the capacitance per unit length remains the same and thus the necessary energy to drive the signal pattern will be the same.

Actually, this scaling has a more troublesome consequence. The signal delay time is proportional to the inverse square of the wire width, since the delay time is proportional to the resistance of the wire per unit length. Even when we make the length of wire short in proportional to the wire width, the delay time does not decrease when we make the width smaller. This is actually yet another way the CMOS scaling law breaks down. Even if the switching speed of the transistors becomes faster, the signal propagation through wires does not.

In order to reduce the energy necessary to access data in the on-chip memory, it is very important to keep the physical distance between a processor core and the memory associated to it sufficiently small. In other words, we are forced to choose a design in which we have many small cores each with small memories. We will return to this problem later.

Our conclusion here is that in principle we can construct a processor with on-chip memory large enough to handle most of problems solved with unstructured mesh, at least with large parallel configurations. When we have to store the data to external DRAM chips, the efficiency of present-day HPC platform is already at the level of a few percents. We believe a system with on-chip memory large enough to store the mesh data, which can solve completely the bandwidth limitation of traditional architecture, is worthwhile to consider. Note that the purpose of the analysis in this chapter is to show that, for each type of numerical methods, it is not impossible to design an architecture on which the power consumption of the arithmetic units is the dominant part of the total power consumption. Thus as far as that goal is concerned, our analysis in this section should suffice.

3.5 Particles

3.5.1 The Overview of Particle-Based Methods

Particle-based simulations have been used in many areas of science and engineering. We can classify these simulations into two categories. In one category, which we could call simulations with real particles, the system is physically a collection of particles as in the case of molecular dynamics, distinct (or discrete) element method (DEM, [32]), or astrophysical simulations of planetary systems, star clusters, galaxies and dark-matter halos. In the other category, the system of partial differential equations for fluid or solid is discretized by particles, which we could call discretization by particles.

In either case, particles interact with other particles. In general, we can express most of particle-based representations of systems as an initial value problem of the following ordinary differential equations:

$$\frac{d\mathbf{u}_i}{dt} = \mathbf{g}\left(\sum_{j}^{N} \mathbf{f}(\mathbf{u}_i, \mathbf{u}_j), \mathbf{u}_i \right). \tag{3.10}$$

Here, N is the number of particles in the system, $\mathbf{u}_i$ is a vector which represents the physical quantities of particle i, $\mathbf{f}$ is a function which describes the contribution of particle j to the time derivative of physical quantities of particle i, and $\mathbf{g}$ is a function which converts the sum of the contributions to the actual time derivative. In the case of gravitational N-body simulation, $\mathbf{u}_i$ contains position, velocity, mass, and other parameters of particle i, $\mathbf{f}$ is the gravitational force from particle j to particle i, and $\mathbf{g}$ gives velocity as the time derivative of position and calculated acceleration as the time derivative of velocity. For many of other problems, $\mathbf{u}_i$ contains position $\mathbf{r}_i$ and velocity $\mathbf{v}_i$, and $\mathbf{f}$ for particles i and j depends on their positions and velocities only through $\mathbf{r}_i - \mathbf{r}_j$ and $\mathbf{v}_i - \mathbf{v}_j$. In addition,

$$\lim_{r_{ij} \to \infty} |\mathbf{f}| = 0, \tag{3.11}$$

where $r_{ij} = |\mathbf{r}_i - \mathbf{r}_j|$. When $|\mathbf{f}|$ decreases only as some power of r_{ij}, we can call $\mathbf{f}$ as a long-range interaction. If $|\mathbf{f}|$ decreases exponentially or has a finite support, we call it a short-range interaction. The most notable example of long-range interactions are gravity and Coulomb interactions, both of which can be expressed by the interaction potential of the form $q_i q_j / r_{ij}$, where q_i is the mass or charge of particle i for gravity and Coulomb interactions, respectively.

Short-range interactions include van-der-Waals force between atoms, force due to physical contact between particles in DEM, interactions between neighboring particles which appear as the result of particle (or meshless) discretization of partial differential equations.

The particle discretization is similar to unstructured mesh, but the main difference is that with the particle discretization we do not have tetrahedron or hexahedron elements which cover the space in a non-overlapping way. As a result, the mathematical basis of the discretization by the particle method is quite different from that of FEM. Actually, there are many different methods for the discretization. For computational fluid dynamics, there are SPH [33] (smoothed particle hydrodynamics) and its infinitely many variations, MPS [34] (Moving Particle Simulation) and its variations, EFGM [35] (Element-Free Galerkin Method), and many others.

In most of particle-based simulations, the cost of the calculation of particle-particle interaction is the dominant part of the total cost. The reason is that the calculation of single pair of calculation is expensive and one particle typically interact with a fair number of particles. The evaluation of the gravity/Coulomb force is one of the simplest interaction. The gravitational force from particle j to particle i is expressed as

$$\mathbf{f}_{ij} = \frac{G m_j m_i \left(\mathbf{r}_j - \mathbf{r}_i\right)}{|\mathbf{r}_j - \mathbf{r}_i|^3}, \qquad (3.12)$$

where m_i, $\mathbf{r}_i$, and $\mathbf{v}_i$, are, the mass, position, and velocity of particle i. Depending on the details of the method to calculate the division and square root, the number of floating-point operations to evaluate and accumulate one interaction is around 30–40. Many modern processors have the instruction to generate the initial guess for the calculation of reciprocal square root, and then the final value is obtained by a several iterations of Newton-Raphson method or schemes with higher-order convergence.

In the case of long-range interactions, one particle feels the forces from all other particles in the system. Thus, the calculation cost of a naive algorithm, in which the force on a particle is actually calculated as the reduction of forces from all other particles, is $O(N^2)$, where N is the number of particles. There are many methods which reduce the calculation cost to $O(N \log N)$ or at least asymptotically $O(N)$, such as the Barnes-Hut tree algorithm [36], the fast multipole method (FMM) [37, 38], particle-particle-particle-mesh (P^{3}M) method [39], and combination of these methods such as TreePM [40, 41].

We first discuss the cost and the memory access of the calculation of the short-range interaction, and then discuss the long-range interaction.

3.5.2 Short-Range Interactions

For short-range interactions, we can extend the idea we used for the structured mesh calculation to evaluate the minimum necessary amount of the memory access. The ideal scheme for structured mesh calculations with explicit and compact schemes should be able to make the memory access per timestep per grid point as close as one read and one write. To achieve this goal, we first read in a block of grid points to on-chip memory, and update all grid points which we can update using the data of grid points in the on-chip memory, and write them back to the external memory. The grid points on the surface of the block cannot be updated, and depending on the width of the finite-difference scheme, a few internal layers of grid points cannot be updated, but the bulk of the grid points can be updated. The additional amount of the memory access thus depends on the amount of the on-chip memory, but can be rather small. This is for the case we do not use the temporal blocking.

In the case of particle-based methods for short-range interaction, we can do exactly the same thing. We divide the particles to overlapping blocks, so that the particles which can be updated cover the entire system, and for each block we read the particles in it to the on-chip memory, and do all necessary calculation to update the updatable particles, and store the updated particles back to the external memory.

The calculation cost per particle per timestep depends primarily on the cutoff length. Particles with distance larger than the cutoff length do not interact through the short-range interaction. The actual form of the cutoff length depends on the problems and schemes used. In some schemes the cutoff length is the same for all particles. In some other schemes, the cutoff length depends on particles but constant during the simulation. In some other method it depends on particles and varies in time. Very roughly speaking, however, the number of particles which one particle interact is of the order of 100–1000, and the minimum number of floating-point operations per interaction is around 30. This minimum is the case of gravity/Coulomb interaction. Thus, for most of short-range interactions, the number of floating-point operations is around 100 or higher, and the minimum number of floating-point operations per particle per timestep is around 10^4. If particles has position, velocity, mass, and a few other variables, the data size is around 50–100 bytes. Thus, we need the memory bandwidth in terms of the B/F number of around 0.01 to balance the speed of the calculation, for particle-based simulation with the minimum calculation cost. For most of practical calculations the necessary memory bandwidth is much smaller.

3.5.3 Long-Range Interactions

For long-range interactions, we can still use the same idea. Here, the idea is to divide the long-range interaction to two terms, the short-range and long-range ones, as is done in the case of P^3M method [39]. Then the short-range part is calculated using the same approach as that of the short-range interaction. The long-range part can be evaluated by a variety of techniques but the calculation cost (and memory access) can be made to be proportional to the number of blocks and independent of the numbers of particles in the blocks. Thus, we can make the cost of the long-range part of the long-range interaction small if the size of the on-chip memory is sufficiently large.

3.6   Random Graphs

In the field of the theoretical analysis of computer networks, random graphs have been extensively studied since they have many very useful characteristics. They have small radii (here, the radius of a graph means the maximum number of nodes between two nodes) for small total number of edges per node. On the other hand, they are rarely used in practice. This is not surprizing, since the routing can be complicated, and the communication can be expensive compared to that on regular networks if the target system has a regular structure. A random graph network can emulate a variety of networks with a near-constant cost, but that cost can be much higher than that for more regular networks.

Thus, random graphs, in their true sense, do not usually appear in large-scale computing. Among the exascale applications, only applications which might be categorized into random graphs are biological neuron simulator and brain simulator. However, the connection of neurons in, for example, the human brain is not at all random but hierarchical.

The total length of axons and dendrites of a human brain is 8.5×10^8 m, and roughly half of that is for Cerebrum. [42]. The total number of neurons in Cerebrum is 1.4×10^{10} and average number of synapses per neuron is 10^4. Thus, the average length of the connection between two neurons is $4 \times 10^8 / 1.4 \times 10^{14} = 3 \times 10^{-6}$ m.

Each neuron has just one long wire (axon). The total length of them in the white matter of a human brain is around 10^5 km [43]. Thus, the typical length of an axon is of the order of 10 mm, which is again much smaller than the size of the brain. In fact, it has been shown that mammal brains can be divided into around 100 areas [44], each with dense internal connections and much less dense inter-area connections.

Thus, we can actually use the idea similar to the temporal blocking we considered in the case of structured mesh calculations, using these areas as the basic units. We can argue that this hierarchical structure is necessary to keep the physical resources used for the wiring in the real brain within the physical limit, and that the nature sees the same limitation as we see. The cost of wiring can be higher than that of transistors or neurons. Of course, the conditions are not exactly the same, since the physical mechanisms of signal propagation and switching are completely different. Even so, we can argue that the typical length of actual wirings, or axons, in natural neural networks, including human brains, is many orders of magnitude shorter than that for a true random graph.

So far, we have only discussed the brains or natural neural networks as the possible example of random graphs, because we could not find other examples in exascale application candidates.

A more theoretical argument would be to apply the concept of the small-world network [45]. The mathematical definition of the small-world network (or graph) is as follows.

A small-world graph is a large-n, sparsely connected, decentralized graph ($n \gg k_{max} \gg 1$) that exhibits a characteristic path length close to that of an equivalent random graph ($L \sim L_{random}$), yet with a clustering coefficient much greater ($C \gg C_{random}$).

Here, n is the number of nodes in the graph, $k_{\max}$ is the maximum number of edges one node has, L is the average "distance" between two nodes where the distance here is measured by the number of edges, and C is the clustering coefficient. The clustering coefficient is defined as the average of C_v over all nodes, and C_v of one node is defined as follows. When a node v has k_v neighbors (nodes connected directly by edges), C_v is defined as the fraction of existing edges between these k_v nodes over $k_v(k_v - 1)/2$.

We can see that for a random graph, even when we require that it is connected, C tends to go to zero for large n. This C does not directly reflect the physical amount of wiring, but clearly related. The fact that many of the actual (both natural and social) networks can be described as small-world networks means that large networks develop hierarchical structures which reduces the number of long connections and thus make it possible to realize them in the physical space.

3.7 Dense Matrices

Operations on large dense matrices, such as the solution of a system of linear equations or calculation of eigenvalues and eigenvectors, can be expressed in terms of matrix-matrix multiplication. For matrix-matrix multiplications, as we have already discussed in Chap. 2, the off-chip memory access can be reduced by a factor proportional to the inverse square root of the size of the on-chip memory and thus can be made very small. Also, some systolic array architecture [46] can be used to reduce the access to on-chip memory. Thus, for applications in which large dense matrices appear, the power consumption is dominated by that of arithmetic units.

Until recently, the main application area of large dense matrices has been quantum chemistry, where the quantum states are described by the eigenvectors. Currently the largest and the most rapidly growing application area of operations on dense matrices is the deep learning. Here, deep learning means the learning using deep neural networks, and "deep" here means the number of layers is large, such as 50 or even larger. Consider a simple network of N layers. The neurons of layer i are connected to all neurons of layer $i - 1$, and the weights of all connections can be changed through the backward error propagation. In this case, the input of layer i, $\mathbf{x}_i$, is expressed as

$$\mathbf{x}_i = A_i \mathbf{y}_{i-1}, \tag{3.13}$$

where A_i is a matrix which gives the weights of connections between layers $i - 1$ and i, and $\mathbf{y}_i$ is the output of layer i. Actual modern networks, for example the convolutional neural networks (CNN), have more complex structure, with only partially dense connections. Even so, the most expensive part of calculations for deep learning applications can be expressed as dense matrix-vector or matrix-matrix multiplications, and the necessary amount of the memory access is very small.

Thus, the processor architecture specialized to deep learning has been the active area of development of commercial products. NVIDIA already has developed three generations of processors (Volta, Turing, Ampere [47]) specialized to deep learning in the sense that they are equipped with specialized circuits for matrix-matrix multiplication. Google also has developed three generations of what they call Tensor Processing Units (TPUs [48]). Intel bought Nervana, a deep learning startup company in 2016 and announced that they would ship products based on Nervana design (SpringCrest), but then they bought yet another deep learning startup, Habana labs, in 2019. Habana Labs announced chips both for inference and learning (Goya and Gaudi). There are many other companies, like Cerebras and Graphcore,

On the other hand, the fact that there are so many projects to develop specialized processors for deep learning, all with different architectures, seem to imply that there isn't a single best solution.

3.8 Summary

In this chapter, we tried to answer two questions we asked at the end of Chap. 2:

1. Can we define a reasonable set of applications for which we want to measure the efficiency of an architecture?
2. For a given application, how we can actually measure and compare the efficiency of different architectures?

For the first question, our answer is that almost all of important applications can be classified to the following five categories

- Structured Mesh
- Unstructured Mesh
- Particles
- "Random" Graphs
- Dense Matrices

An important observation is that we do not really deal with true "random graphs", for which efficient parallel computation would be very hard. In practice, many of actual large networks, no matter they are natural, social or artificial, have the characteristics of the small-world network, which means large fraction of connections are localized. Thus, computational characteristics of "random" graphs is not much different from that of unstructured mesh.

Our answer to the first question is not that we can specify the set of applications, but that we can specify a set of categories of applications. It is dangerous to specify an application program (or benchmark code) as the representative of a category, since the way the actual programs are written depends on the available hardware and software, and thus not necessarily represent the best possible way.

As an example, consider a computational fluid dynamics calculation on a regular grid using compressive and explicit numerical scheme. Traditional codes are written for vector-parallel machines, and thus require rather high memory bandwidth (the B/F number of around four). In theory, as we discussed, we can reduce the required memory bandwidth of explicit schemes by a large factor, to the B/F number of around 0.01 or less, if the size of the on-chip memory is large enough. However, with existing processors it is very difficult or impossible to reduce the main memory access, even when they are equipped with large cache memories, because the structure of the cache memory prevents its effective utilization.

Thus, our analysis should be somewhat more abstract, assuming the existence of an ideal processor architecture, with which the data transfer between the arithmetic units, on-chip memory, and off-chip memory can be reduced to what is theoretically necessary. This assumption might looks too optimistic, and we'll see if we can actually design such processors in Chap. 5

With this assumption, the answer to the second question turned out to be simple. With the optimal design for connections between arithmetic units, on-chip memory, and off-chip memory, for all of the above application categories the power consumption of the arithmetic units should dominate over the power consumption of memory units or the movement of data between units. Again, this conclusion probably looks like an oversimplification. We will see if we can actually design such a processor in Chap. 5

Thus, our definition of the efficiency of a computer architecture for a given application class is simple. The power efficiency of a processor is defined as the ratio of the power consumed in the combinatorial logic of arithmetic units, assuming that the operation is done in the necessary accuracy, to its total power consumption. Similarly, we can define the area or transistor efficiency as the fraction of the silicon die or transistors of the processor used for the combinatorial logic of the arithmetic units.

Note that our definition of the efficiency only specifies the efficiency in the usage of electricity and silicon real estate (or transistor count) for a given semiconductor technology (and also given supply voltage), and thus cannot be used to compare processors made with different technology. On the other hand, the reduction of the power consumption through the miniaturization of transistors has slowed down, and the fabrication cost of transistors is now going up. Therefore, even though the actual power consumption and fabrication cost can depend on the device technology used, that variation is smaller than it used to be.

In the next chapter, we try to measure the processors in the past from our viewpoints of the efficiency.

References

1. Y. Sabharwal, S. Garg, G. R., J. Gunnels, R. Sahoo, in *High Performance Computing (HiPC 2008)*. *HiPC 2008*. Lecture Notes in Computer Science, vol. 5374. (Springer, Berlin, 2008). Lecture Notes in Computer Science
2. R. Egawa, K. Komatsu, S. Momose, Y. Isobe, A. Musa, H. Takizawa, H. Kobayashi, J. Supercomput. **73**(9), 3948 (2017). https://doi.org/10.1007/s11227-017-1993-y
3. T. Ishiyama, K. Nitadori, J. Makino, in *Proceedings of the International Conference on High Performance Computing, Networking, Storage and Analysis (SC '12)* (IEEE Computer Society Press, Los Alamitos, 2012), pp. 5:1–5:10. http://dl.acm.org/citation.cfm?id=2388996.2389003
4. M. Iwasawa, A. Tanikawa, N. Hosono, K. Nitadori, T. Muranushi, J. Makino, Publ. Astron. Soc. Jpn. **68**, 54 (2016). https://doi.org/10.1093/pasj/psw053
5. K. Chiba, A. Okada, Y. Shiraishi, Genomon. https://genomon.readthedocs.io
6. H. Li, R. Durbin, Bioinformatics **25**(14), 1754 (2009). https://doi.org/10.1093/bioinformatics/btp324
7. M. Burrows, D.J. Wheeler, A block-sorting lossless data compression algorithm. Tech. Rep. SRC-RR-124 (Digital Equipment Corporation Systems Research Center, California, 1994). https://www.hpl.hp.com/techreports/Compaq-DEC/SRC-RR-124.html
8. S. Lele, J. Comput. Phys. **103**(1), 16 (1992). https://doi.org/10.1016/0021-9991(92)90324-R. Cited By 4542
9. M. Rempel, Astrophys. J. **622**(2), 1320 (2005). https://doi.org/10.1086/428282
10. H. Hotta, M. Rempel, T. Yokoyama, Y. Iida, Y. Fan, Astron. Astrophys. **539**, A30 (2012). https://doi.org/10.1051/0004-6361/201118268
11. M. Eleftheriou, J. Moreira, R. Fitch, B.G. Germain, in *HiPC 2003*. Lecture Notes in Computer Science, vol. 2913 (Springer, Berlin, 2003), pp. 194–203
12. A. Chan, W. Balaji, P. Gropp, R. Thakur, in *HiPC 2008*. Lecture Notes in Computer Science, vol. 5374 (Springer, Berlin, 2008), pp. 350–364
13. D. Takahashi, in *Parallel Processing and Applied Mathematics*. Lecture Notes in Computer Science, vol. 6067 (Springer, Berlin, 2010), pp. 606–614
14. D. Takahashi, A. Uno, M. Yokokawa, in *Proceedings of the 2012 IEEE 14th International Conference on High Performance Computing and Communication 2012 IEEE 9th International Conference on Embedded Software and Systems* (2012), pp. 344–350
15. M. Yokokawa, K. Itakura, A. Uno, T. Ishihara, Y. Kaneda, in *Proceedings of the 2002 ACM/IEEE conference on Supercomputing* (IEEE Computer Society, New York, 2002), pp. 1–17
16. H. Tanaka, Y. Ishihara, R. Sakamoto, T. Nakamura, Y. Kimura, K. Nitadori, M. Tsubouchi, J. Makino, in *Proceedings of the 2018 IEEE/ACM 4th International Workshop on Extreme Scale Programming Models and Middleware (ESPM2)* (2018), pp. 29–36
17. M. Wolfe, in *Proceedings Supercomputing '89* (IEEE, Los Alamitos, 1989), pp. 655–664
18. J. Ragan-Kelley, C. Barnes, A. Adams, S. Paris, F. Durand, S. Amarasinghe, ACM SIGPLAN Not. **48**(6), 519 (2013)
19. T. Muranushi, J. Makino, Procedia Comput. Sci. **51**, 1303 (2015)
20. S.S. Rao, *The Finite Element Method in Engineering*, 6th edn. (Elsevier, Amsterdam, 2018)
21. A. Brandt, Math. Comput. **31**(138), 333 (1977). http://www.jstor.org/stable/2006422
22. A.V.D. Sluis, H.V.D. Vorst, Numer. Math. **48**, 543 (1986). http://eudml.org/doc/133086
23. H.A. Van der Vorst, K. Dekker, J. Comput. Appl. Math. **24**(1), 73 (1988). https://doi.org/10.1016/0377-0427(88)90344-5. http://www.sciencedirect.com/science/article/pii/0377042788903445
24. J.J. Dongarra, A. Heroux, Michael, P. Luszczek, HPCG benchmark: a new metric for ranking high performance computing systems. Tech. Rep. 15-736 (Department of Electrical Engineering and Computer Science, University of Tennessee System, Knoxville, 2015). http://www.eecs.utk.edu/resources/library/594

25. HPCG Project Team, June 2020 HPCG results (2020). http://www.hpcg-benchmark.org/custom/index.html?lid=155&slid=303
26. I. Babuška, H. Elman, J. Comput. Appl. Math. **27**(1), 157 (1989). https://doi.org/10.1016/0377-0427(89)90365-8. http://www.sciencedirect.com/science/article/pii/0377042789903658. Special Issue on Parallel Algorithms for Numerical Linear Algebra
27. G.F. Carey, B.N. Jiang, Commun. Appl. Numer. Methods **2**(2), 145 (1986). https://doi.org/10.1002/cnm.1630020205. https://onlinelibrary.wiley.com/doi/abs/10.1002/cnm.1630020205
28. G.F. Carey, E. Barragy, R. McLay, M. Sharma, Commun. Appl. Numer. Methods **4**(3), 299 (1988). https://doi.org/10.1002/cnm.1630040303. https://onlinelibrary.wiley.com/doi/abs/10.1002/cnm.1630040303
29. M. LaPedus, TSMC devises sram cell at 28-nm (2009). https://www.eetimes.com/tsmc-devises-sram-cell-at-28-nm/
30. G. Yeap, S.S. Lin, Y.M. Chen, H.L. Shang, P.W. Wang, H.C. Lin, Y.C. Peng, J.Y. Sheu, M. Wang, X. Chen, B.R. Yang, C.P. Lin, F.C. Yang, Y.K. Leung, D.W. Lin, C.P. Chen, K.F. Yu, D.H. Chen, C.Y. Chang, H.K. Chen, P. Hung, C.S. Hou, Y.K. Cheng, J. Chang, L. Yuan, C.K. Lin, C.C. Chen, Y.C. Yeo, M.H. Tsai, H.T. Lin, C.O. Chui, K.B. Huang, W. Chang, H.J. Lin, K.W. Chen, R. Chen, S.H. Sun, Q. Fu, H.T. Yang, H.T. Chiang, C.C. Yeh, T.L. Lee, C.H. Wang, S.L. Shue, C.W. Wu, R. Lu, W.R. Lin, J. Wu, F. Lai, Y.H. Wu, B.Z. Tien, Y.C. Huang, L.C. Lu, J. He, Y. Ku, J. Lin, M. Cao, T.S. Chang, S.M. Jang, in *Proceedings of the 2019 IEEE International Electron Devices Meeting (IEDM)* (2019), pp. 36.7.1–36.7.4
31. I. Bahl, P. Bhartia, *Microwave Solid State Circuit Design*, 2nd edn. (Wiley, New York, 2003)
32. P.A. Cundall, O.D. Strack, Geotechnique **29**(1), 47 (1979)
33. R.A. Gingold, J.J. Monaghan, Mon. Not. R. Astron. Soc. **181**, 375 (1977)
34. S. Koshizuka, Y. Oka, Nucl. Sci. Eng. **123**(3), 421 (1996). https://doi.org/10.13182/NSE96-A24205
35. T. Belytschko, Y.Y. Lu, L. Gu, Int. J. Numer. Methods Eng. **37**(2), 229 (1994). https://doi.org/10.1002/nme.1620370205. https://onlinelibrary.wiley.com/doi/abs/10.1002/nme.1620370205
36. J. Barnes, P. Hut, Nature **324**, 446 (1986)
37. V. Rokhlin, J. Comput. Phys. **60**, 187 (1983)
38. L. Greengard, V. Rokhlin, in *Vortex Methods*, ed. by C. Anderson, C. Greengard. Lecture Notes in Mathematics, vol. 1360 (Springer, Berlin, 1988), pp. 121–141
39. R.W. Hockney, J.W. Eastwood, *Computer Simulation Using Particles* (IOP Publishing Ltd., Bristol, 1988)
40. J.S. Bagla, J. Astrophys. Astron. **23**, 185 (2002). https://doi.org/10.1007/BF02702282
41. T. Ishiyama, T. Fukushige, J. Makino, Publ. Astron. Soc. Jpn. **61**, 1319 (2009)
42. T. McCaslin, K. Grace, P. Christiano, Transmitting fibers in the brain: Total length and distribution of lengths (2018). https://aiimpacts.org/transmitting-fibers-in-the-brain-total-length-and-distribution-of-lengths/
43. L. Marner, J.R. Nyengaard, Y. Tang, B. Pakkenberg, J. Comp. Neurol. **462**(2), 144 (2003). https://doi.org/10.1002/cne.10714. https://onlinelibrary.wiley.com/doi/abs/10.1002/cne.10714
44. C. Kerepesi, B. Szalkai, B. Varga, V. Grolmusz, Neurosci. Lett. **662**, 17 (2018). https://www.sciencedirect.com/science/article/abs/pii/S0304394017308212
45. D.J. Watts, Am. J. Sociol. **105**(2), 493 (1999). https://doi.org/10.1086/210318
46. H. Kung, C. Leiserson, *Introduction to VLSI Systems* (1980). Cited By 228
47. NVIDIA Corporation, Nvidia a100 tensor core GPU architecture (2020). https://www.nvidia.com/content/dam/en-zz/Solutions/Data-Center/nvidia-ampere-architecture-whitepaper.pdf
48. N.P. Jouppi, C. Young, N. Patil, D. Patterson, G. Agrawal, R. Bajwa, S. Bates, S. Bhatia, N. Boden, A. Borchers, R. Boyle, P.l. Cantin, C. Chao, C. Clark, J. Coriell, M. Daley, M. Dau, J. Dean, B. Gelb, T.V. Ghaemmaghami, R. Gottipati, W. Gulland, R. Hagmann, C.R. Ho, D. Hogberg, J. Hu, R. Hundt, D. Hurt, J. Ibarz, A. Jaffey, A. Jaworski, A. Kaplan, H. Khaitan, D. Killebrew, A. Koch, N. Kumar, S. Lacy, J. Laudon, J. Law, D. Le, C. Leary, Z. Liu,

K. Lucke, A. Lundin, G. MacKean, A. Maggiore, M. Mahony, K. Miller, R. Nagarajan, R. Narayanaswami, R. Ni, K. Nix, T. Norrie, M. Omernick, N. Penukonda, A. Phelps, J. Ross, M. Ross, A. Salek, E. Samadiani, C. Severn, G. Sizikov, M. Snelham, J. Souter, D. Steinberg, A. Swing, M. Tan, G. Thorson, B. Tian, H. Toma, E. Tuttle, V. Vasudevan, R. Walter, W. Wang, E. Wilcox, D.H. Yoon, SIGARCH Comput. Archit. News **45**(2), 1–12 (2017). https://doi.org/10.1145/3140659.3080246

Chapter 4
Analysis of Past and Present Processors

History teaches.

— Gertrude Stein

In this chapter, we analyze past and present processors from the viewpoint of the efficiency we defined in Chap. 3.

4.1 CDC 6600

First we consider the CDC 6600 [1]. The total number of transistors used for CDC 6600 is 400,000. The basic logic element used in 6600 is DCTL (direct coupled transistor logic). In DCTL, the NOT gate uses one transistor and both AND and OR gates use two transistors (both with several resistors). Modern CMOS NOT and NAND gates use two and four transistors (FETs). Thus, if we follow the usual convention of counting four CMOS FETs as one gate, 6600 consists of 200 K gates. Each gates consumes around 0.05 W at its 10 MHz operation, and thus the power consumption of the CPU of CDC 6600 is around 10 KW.

The entire CDC 6600 consists of 16 chassis, each of which can hold 756 modules. One module consists of two printed-circuit boards. Out of 16 chassis, eights are used for the main memory made of magnetic cores, and one is not used. Thus, the remaining seven units are used for logic circuits of CPU, PPU (peripheral control unit) and peripherals. Five chassis are used for CPU, and add-shift, divide, multiply, register and control units are assigned to these five chassis. Thus, very roughly speaking 1/7 of the total logic circuits are used for floating-point multiplication units.

The arithmetic units of 6600 are not pipelined, but designed to give results using multiple clock cycles (what is called "minor cycles" in [1]). It has two multipliers each of which can produce one result in every 10 clock periods (major cycles). Thus, the total throughput is 0.2 results per clock period. The multiplier logic for the mantissa need four iterations to obtain all partial sums, and the mantissa of 6600

© Springer Nature Switzerland AG 2021
J. Makino, *Principles of High-Performance Processor Design*,
https://doi.org/10.1007/978-3-030-76871-3_4

is 48 bits. Thus, effectively one multiplier should have 12 48-bit carry-save adders, or 576 full adders. It also require at least four 48-bit flip-flops. If we assume, as in the case of CMOS logic, both one full adder and one flip-flops require 10 gates, the total gate count of one multiplier unit of 6600 is 7680, and the transistor count should be around 16 k for one multiplier and 32 k for the two units implemented in 6600. This is around 1/12 of the total transistor count of 6600, and thus somewhat smaller than the transistor count we can guess from the fact that they occupy one chassis (1/7). On the other hand, there is no reason to believe each chassis contain exactly 1/7 of total number of transistors. Therefore we believe that our estimate that 1/12 of the total transistors are used for multipliers is reasonable.

It should be noted that if a fully pipelined multiplier had been implemented, it would consume $48 \times 48 = 2304$ full adders or around 46 K transistors. The throughput would be five times higher than that of two units of 6600, for 1.5 times more transistors. Thus, such a design would be three times more efficient. Therefore, the effective fraction of the circuits used for floating-point multipliers is 46,000/5/400,000 or 2.3%.

We should take into account the logic for the floating-point addition. The main logic units of a floating-point adder are two shifters (one of two inputs and output) and one adder. Each shifter would consists of six stages of multiplexers, each with 1.5 gates in CMOS which add up to around 1000 gates. A fast carry-look-ahead or carry-select adder would consume another 100–1500 gates. Thus the total gate count for a double-precision floating-point adder is around 2500 gates, or 5 K transistors in DCTL. It is probably reasonable to assume that the size of the combinatorial logic of the double-precision floating-point adder is 10–20% of that of the multiplier. If we take the somewhat conservative number of 20%, we can conclude that the effective fraction of logic transistors used for the floating-point arithmetic unit of 6600 is 2.8%.

In the case of DCTL logic, one gate consumes a constant amount of power independent of the clock frequency. Thus, we can assume that the transistor efficiency and the power efficiency are the same. In both meanings, the efficiency of 6600 is 2.8%.

One might think this number is too small to be true or useful. However, we will see that many of modern processors have even lower efficiencies. In fact, at its time, 6600 had rather high fraction of logic used for arithmetic circuits. The section for multiply unit of [1] starts with:

> Two identical Multiply Units are included in the 6600 Central Processor. While this is small extravagance, the use of multiplication, particularly in multiple precision computation, represents a large percentage of time.

Thus, both the designer of the machine and the author of the book quite correctly understood the importance of the arithmetic logic, while even at 1970. having two multipliers could be regarded as "extravagance". Of course, the choice to have this extravagance is how 6600 became the fastest computer in the world.

4.2 Cray-1 and Its Successors

Cray-1 [2] was designed with small-scale integrated circuits (SSIs). The basic components are

- dual NAND gates of five and four inputs
- dual D flip-flops (DFF)
- 16×4 bit register file
- $4k \times 1$ bit RAM

With SSIs, the relationship between the size of the circuits and the number of transistors can be rather complicated, since the number of transistors in one logic gate chip, one register file chip, and one SRAM chip are quite different. In the CMOS design, the dual NAMD gate chip requires 18 transistors, One DFF 4 transmission gates and 4 NOT gates, or around 6.5 gates = 23 transistors, and thus SSI with two DFFs 46 transistors. A memory cell would use six transistors and thus 16×4 bit register file requires around 400 transistors, and $4k \times 1$ bit SRAM 24 k transistors. Thus, register file chips can contain transistors 10 times more than those in logic chips, and SRAM chips many orders more. This characteristics of register file (and SRAM) chips made a large set of registers relatively inexpensive.

On modern VLSI chip, the difference is much smaller, except for the case of off-chip DRAMs.

Table 4.1 gives the detailed gate counts for each of the functional units of Cray-1S [2]. Here, the total gate count is 75,259. At the same time, the total gate count of Cray-1S is 230,000 [2]. Thus, only 1/3 of the total gates is used for functional units and remaining 2/3 is used for control and data path.

Table 4.1 Cray-1S gate counts [2]

Functional units	Gate count	Percentage of total
Address adder	1952	2.59
Address multiply	4009	5.33
Scalar add	2968	3.94
Scalar single shift	1452	1.93
Scalar double shift	2976	3.95
Constant to Si	482	0.64
Pop and zero count to Ai	403	0.54
Vector integer add	2216	2.94
Vector logical	1984	2.64
Vector shift	3460	4.60
Vector pop count	490	0.65
Floating add	8247	11.0
Floating multiply	23,116	30.7
Reciprocal	21,504	28.6
Total	75,259	100.0

The total number of PCB boards is 1152 and each PCB board can hold up to 144 SSI chips, and 95% of the SSI chips are NAND gates and remaining 5% are DFF and register files. Thus, there could be up to 150 K NAND gate chips, for the total gate count of 300 K, which is consistent with the 230 K number mentioned above. Therefore, the total number of NAND gate chips should be around 100 K.

Cray-1 has eight 64-words, 64-bit vector registers. This register file would require 197 k transistors, but can be implemented with only 512 register file chips. On the other hands, floating-point adder and multiplier use 31,363 gates in total, which means about 16 K logic chips.

A 6×8 multiplier is constructed using 110 SSI chips or 220 gates. The gate count in the modern sense would be 48 FAs and 480 gates. Thus, we can regard one "gate" in Cray-1 as equivalent to around two gates in the modern sense. Thus, the total number of gates, in the modern sense, used for the floating-point adder and multiplier is 60 k. which is about a factor of two larger than the minimum necessary number of around 30 k. The fraction of the gate used for these two units is $30/230 = 13\%$, and with the correction factor of two, the effective fraction of logic gates used for floating-point adder and multiplier is 6.5%. We can see this number is significantly larger than that of CDC 6600. The main reason is the move from the architecture with non-pipelined multiple function units to that with single fully-pipelined unit. The raw fraction of transistors used for function units are rather similar, probably reflecting the principle of the main designer.

The architectures of Cray X-MP and Y-MP are essentially the same as that of Cray-1, except for the memory interface and interprocessor connection. Thus, the gate count and fraction of the gate used for floating-point arithmetic units are also very similar to that of Cray-1.

The Cray-2 [3] uses 165,000 16-gate chips. The meaning of gate here is not clear, but if we assume that it is close to the modern sense, we can see that the total gate count of 2M is close to for times that of Cray-1 (460 k in modern sense). Thus, even with Cray-2, the fraction of the gates used for floating-point arithmetic logic is not much different from that of Cray-1.

We should note that Cray vector machines are designed under the assumption of abundant memory bandwidth, and thus do not have the data cache. As a result, compared to modern processors with hierarchical cache memories, The design of Cray vector machines looks efficient in terms of the transistor count. In that sense, their design was made with the assumption which is not valid today. Even so, the analysis of them are useful because it tells us what can be done if very high memory bandwidth is available.

4.3   x86 Processors

4.3.1   i860

The first Intel processor which was designed for heavy workloads with floating-point calculation, i860 [4], is not one of x86 processors, though its name suggests otherwise. Even though it is not an x86 processor, i860 occupies a very important position in the history of microprocessors. It is the first single-chip superscalar RISC processor with a heavily (albeit not fully) pipelined floating-point arithmetic unit.

The transistor count of i860 is 1 million [5]. It is fabricated using $1\,\mu m$ technology and its die size is $10\,mm \times 15\,mm$. The transistor count of the second-generation i860XP is 2.55 million [6]. It is fabricated using $0.8\,\mu m$ technology and its die size is $10.3\,mm \times 15.5\,mm$. The main difference between two processors is in the size of I- and D-caches. The i860 has 4 KB I-cache and 8 KB D-cache, while with i860XP both of I- and D-caches are increased to 16 KB.

If we assume that usual six-transistor cells are used for the caches, the numbers of transistors used for the caches are 586 k and 1536 k, for i860 and i860XP, respectively. this means that the number of the transistors used for the CPU core logic is 410 k and 1M for i860 and i860XP, respectively. This is roughly consistent with what we can see from the photo of two dies (Fig. 4.1), in which the core logic of i860XP is identical to that of i860 except the additional logic to the left. Apparently the transistors used for the core logic of i860XP is around 50% higher than that of i860. The size of the cache tag region might have slight non-linearity to the cache size. Therefore we believe the estimate of 410 K transistors for the CPU core logic is reasonable.

From Fig. 4.1 we can estimate that floating point multiplier and adder occupy around 1/3 of the total real estate used for the CPU core. Very roughly, we can estimate the total number of transistors used is 130 k. This number is about the same as the minimum necessary number of transistors necessary for the combinatorial logic circuits for them. A factor of two could come from additional circuits for pipeline registers and also from the fact that the n-cycle multiplier has the size significantly larger than $1/n$ of the fully pipeline multiplier. Thus, the raw fraction of total transistors on chip used for the FP logic is 13% for the original i860, and if we apply the correction factor of two, it would be 6.5%. For the second generation i860XP, these numbers are 5.1% and 2.6%.

We can see that these numbers are rather close to what we observed for CDC 6600 and Cray-1.

The memory bandwidth of i860 processors is very high. The memory data bus is of 64-bit width, and can transfer one 64-bit data in every two clock cycles. In this two clock cycles, the CPU core can do one FMA operation. Thus i860 has B/F of 4.

Fig. 4.1 The Intel i860(left) and i860XP (right) processors. The physical sizes of two chips are roughly the same. Here, the sizes are scaled so that the size of the corresponding functional units are similar. Author: Pauli Rautakorpi This file is licensed under the Creative Commons Attribution 3.0 Unported license. Taken from https://en.wikipedia.org/wiki/File:Intel_i860XR_die.JPG and https://commons.wikimedia.org/wiki/File:Intel_i860XP_die.JPG

4.3.2   From Pentium to Skylake

Table 4.2 and Fig. 4.2 show the evolution of Intel x86 processors from Pentium (1993) to Skylake Xeon (2017). The left-top panel of Fig. 4.2 shows the total number of transistors including the transistors for cache memories, N_{trs}, the right-top panel the effective number of FMA units per processor, N_{FMA}. Here, the effective number of FMA units is defined as the maximum number of FMA operations executable per clock cycle. The bottom panel shows the transistor efficiency, which we define as

$$\eta_{\text{trs}} = N_{\text{tpF}} \frac{N_{\text{FMA}}}{N_{\text{trs}}}, \tag{4.1}$$

Table 4.2 Year of introduction, total number of transistors and the number of FMA-equivalent operations per clock cycle of Intel x86 processors

Processor	Year	# of transistors	FMAs/clock
Pentium	1993	3.1M	0.5
Pentium Pro	1995	5.5M	0.5
Pentium II	1997	7.5M	0.5
Pentium III	1999	9.5M	0.5
Pentium 4	2002	42M	1
Core 2 Duo E6300	2006	291M	4
Core 2 Xeon E7450	2008	1.9G	12
Nehalem Core i7-850	2009	774M	8
Nehalem Xeon E7-2850	2011	2.6G	20
Sandy Bridge Core i7-2600	2011	1160M	16
Ivy Bridge Xeon E5-2695v2	2013	4.3G	48
Haswell Core i7-4790	2013	1400M	32
Broadwell Xeon E5-2696v3	2014	7.2G	176
KNL Xeon Phi	2016	7.1G	1152
Skylake Xeon Platinum 8180	2017	8G	448

where N_{tpF} is the number of transistors necessary for the combinatorial logic of one FMA unit. We assume $N_{tpF} = 120,000$.

In 24 years, the number of transistors in one processor chip increased by a factor of 2,600 from 3.1M to 8G, while the number of FMA units increased by a factor of 900 from 0.5 to 448. The largest number, 1152, is for the Xeon Phi processor, which is not regarded as a great commercial success. The main reason of the failure is its rather low performance for many of real applications. Therefore it is better to regard this processor as exceptional.

We can see that the increase of a factor of 600 in the transistor count took place in the first 15 years, from 1993 to 2008, and another factor of four in the remaining 9 years. Actually, even at year 2021, the largest single-die processor from Intel still have 28 cores, and based on the same 14 nm process as used in the processor in 2017. Therefore we can say this increase of a factor of 4 is for 12 years. In any case, there is a drastic slowdown in the increase of the transistor count. First Pentium of 1993 was fabricated using 0.8 μm BiCMOS process, Xeon E7450 of 2008 45 nm process, and Xeon Platinum of 2017 (and 2021) uses 14 nm process. If the process rule gives the accurate linear size of transistors, 45 nm process should allow 320 times more transistors compared to 0.8 μm process, and 14 nm process 10 times more transistors compared to 45 nm process. Actual increases are of factors of 600 and four, respectively. We can see that the nominal number in the process rule is not reliable for recent processes, in particular after 22 nm process where the FinFET structure was adopted.

On the other hand, the increases of the number of FMAs started in 2000, and a factor of 20 increase occurred by 2008, and another factor of 20 increase occurred

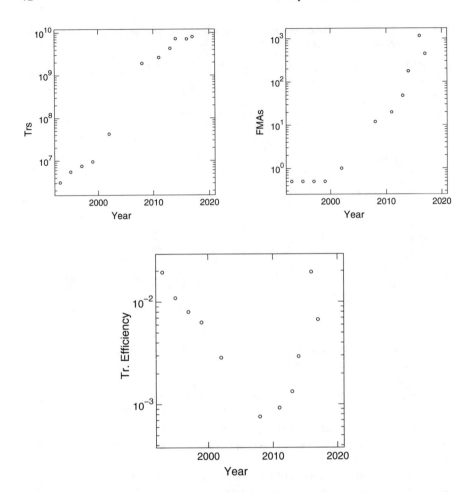

Fig. 4.2 The total number of transistors (top left), the effective number of FMA units (top right), and the number of transistors per one FMA unit, of representative Intel x86 microprocessors

by 2017. As a result, the transistor efficiency went down from 2% of Pentium to 0.08% of Xeon E7450, and went up by a factor of 10 to 0.8% of Xeon Platinum.

The improvement of the transistor efficiency came from the increase of the number of FMA units per core. Core 2 Xeon had one SSE4 unit, which could perform two multiplications and two additions in parallel. Thus, the number of FMAs per core was two. The number of FMA units per core of the Nehalem architecture was the same two, but processor cores of Sandy(Ivy)Bridge, Has(Broad)well and Skylake architectures supported AVX, AVX2, and AVX512 instruction set, and performed 4, 8, and 16 FMAs per clock cycles, respectively. This increase of a factor of eight almost completely explain the factor of nine increase in the transistor efficiency from Core 2 architecture to Skylake architecture.

Apparently, right now it is difficult to further improve the efficiency of Intel x86 processors, or actually any multicore CPU architecture with coherent hierarchical caches and SIMD execution units. This is most clearly visible from the fact that the recent Intel processor with the highest transistor efficiency, Xeon Phi, turned out to be the failure and its development was canceled in 2017. Even though the transistor efficiency of Xeon Phi is much higher than that of mainstream Xeon processors, the actual gain in the performance was for many programs not large. Another indication is that AMD adopted multi-die, NUMA architecture for its EPYC processor line. The main advantage of NUMA architecture is simply that we can reduce the number of long wires within the processor chip.

There are two main differences between the architectures of Xeon Phi and mainstream Xeon. One is that Xeon Phi lacks the on-chip level-3 cache. Thus, the performance penalty of L2D cache miss is very large. On the other hand, the size of L2D cache is not large, just 1 MB shared by two cores, and Xeon Phi lacks low-latency communication mechanism between cores. As a result, it is difficult to efficiently parallelize application programs. In order to avoid the large penalty caused by communication or just barrier synchronization, parallelization using MPI would be preferred over that by OpenMP, even though the large number of cores share the same physical memory. However, with such parallelization, the size of L2 cache per core is too small to hide the large latency and small bandwidth of the main memory.

The second difference is in the processor core. The processor core of Xeon Phi is based on Intel's Silvermont and Airmont architecture used for Atom processors. Compared to the processor core used for Xeon (such as Haswell and Skylake), they have much weaker out-of-order execution capability. In particular, their instruction decoder has the throughput of two instructions per cycle (two-way decoder). In comparison, all Xeon processors after Core architecture, up to Haswell, have four-way decoders, and the Skylake microarchitecture has a five-way decoder. As we have seen in Sect. 4.1, even a simple loop requires three or more instructions issued and executed in parallel to fully utilize a pipelined FP unit. Thus, it is not surprising that the efficiency of Xeon Phi is significantly lower than that of mainstream Xeon.

In addition, the power efficiency of Xeon Phi turned out to be not much different from that of the mainstream Xeon fabricated using the same process technology. In the Top500 list of November 2016, the highest performance per watt number for Xeon Phi (KNL) was 6.05 Gflops/W, but most other KNL-based systems reached only 4.5–5.0 Gflops/W. On the other hand, Skylake-based systems in the June 2018 list reached 4.5 Gflops/W. Thus, even though the application efficiency can be very different, the power efficiency, when running at near-peak performance, are not much different. The fact the power efficiency of Xeon and Xeon Phi is similar is actually somewhat difficult to understand, considering the fact that Xeon has much more rich cores and cache hierarchy. One possibility is that the design of the FP unit itself determines the total power consumption. The AVX512 instruction set supports a large variety of permute and table lookup functions, which makes flexible reordering within one AVX512 register possible. These function require large and power-consuming circuit, which makes the total area of the FP unit larger, resulting in the further increase of the power consumption. As we have already seen in Sect. 2.1.5, on modern VLSI processors the movement of data can consume more power than the actual computation, even within one processor core.

Thus, Xeon Phi seems to indicate that it is difficult to further improve the efficiency of CPUs. The strategies followed by Intel Xeon processors are

1. Increase the number of cores in one chip, keeping the architecture of physically shared main memory.
2. Increase the width of the SIMD execution units in one core, keeping the number of units small (one or two)
3. Add the levels of cache memories to hide the latency and bandwidth limitation of the main memory.

Among these three strategies, only the second one contributed to the improvement of the transistor efficiency. The first and third ones are more like the response to the increase of the available number of transistors, and do not directly contribute to the improvement of the efficiency in any way. In fact, they have negative impact on the application efficiency.

In Broadwell and Skylake architectures, each core can execute two load and one write instructions per cycle. Thus the B/F number of the L1D cache is six. Note that this is not enough to achieve the peak performance for DAXPY or inner product operations, since these processors have two FP units. Even so, this quite high bandwidth of the L1 cache is one of the many reasons for the large power consumption of processors of x86 architecture. The bandwidth between L1 and L2 is 52 bytes per cycle, and that between L2 and L3 is 15 bytes per cycle [7]. From the viewpoint of the effective use of FP units, high bandwidth, low latency caches are desirable. On the other hand, from the viewpoint of the energy and transistor efficiency, lower bandwidth and higher latency are desirable. We will see how a different design decision changes the energy and transistor efficiency in the next section.

4.4 NEC SX-Aurora and Fujitsu A64fx

In the previous section we have seen that it is difficult to increase the SIMD width further with the current structure and instruction set of Intel x86 architecture. One possibility is to move (back) to the vector architecture [8, 9]. The NEC SX-Aurora processor [9] integrates 10 processor cores, each with 96 FMA units. The total number of transistors used is unknown, but the SX-Aurora processor is fabricated using TSMC 16 nm technology and the chip size is not excessively large (500 mm^2). Thus, compared to Skylake Xeon or even Xeon Phi, it is probably more transistor efficient. On the other hand, the total power consumption seems to be similar.

Figure 4.3 gives the block diagram of the NEC SX-Aurora processor. The clock frequency is 1.6 GHz. Thus, one core has the peak performance of 307.2 Gflops. In the case of the traditional vector processors, such as Cray machines or Japanese

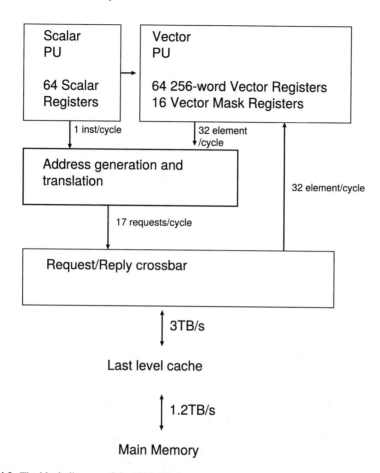

Fig. 4.3 The block diagram of the NEC SX-Aurora processor

machines in 1980s, B/F=4 was maintained. If same B/F=4 were maintained with SX-Aurora, the bandwidth between registers and memory would be 1228 GB/s (read and write added). With 10 processors, this means one would need the last level cache bandwidth of 12.3 TB/s. The actual total bandwidth of LLC is 3 TB/s, and the memory bandwidth is further reduced to 1.2 TB/s. Thus the nominal B/F number of the LLC is 1.0 and that of the main memory is 0.4.

Figure 4.4 gives the block diagram of the Fujitsu A64fx processor [10]. The clock frequency is 2 or 2.2 GHz. Each core has two 512-bit wide SIMD units, each of which can perform eight double-precision FMA operations per cycle. Thus, one core has the peak performance of 70.4 Gflops for 2.2 GHz clock. Either two loads or one store instructions can be executed in one cycle. The bandwidth between L1D cache and L2D cache is 1024 GB/s or 512 GB/s for read/write, shared by 12 cores. These 12 cores and one L2D cache form what Fujitsu named CMG (Core-Memory group). One CMG is connected to one HBM2 memory with the peak transfer rate

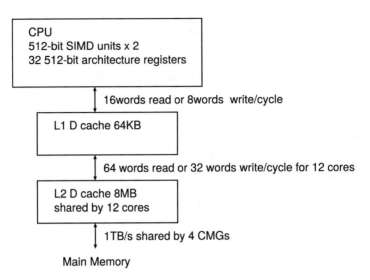

Fig. 4.4 The block diagram of the Fujitsu A64fx processor

of 256 GB/s, and CMGs are connected in a ring network with the bandwidth of
115 GB/s. The B/F number of the L2D cache is 1.3 and that of the main memory is
0.30.

We can see that even though the architectures of these two processors are quite
different, the structures and throughputs of the memory hierarchy are rather similar.
Both processors have the peak performance of around 3TF, bandwidth between the
first- and second level memory (L1D and L2D for A64fx, and vector registers and
the LLC for SX-Aurora) of around 3 TB/s, and the external memory bandwidth of
1 TB/s. The total amount of L1D cache of A64fx is 3.07 MB, while the total size of
the vector registers of SX-Aurora is 1.28 MB. The sizes of L2D of A64fx and LLC
of SX-Aurora are 32 MB and 20 MB.

If we compare A64fx with Intel Skylake, we observe the following difference

- L1D throughput of A64fx is one half of that of Skylake.
- L2D write throughput is 40% of that of Skylake.
- External memory throughput is more than two times higher than that of Skylake.

There are also difference in the amount of out-of-order resources. Skylake has
quite a bit mote resource for reorder buffer and renaming registers. Whether or not
these differences cause significant difference in the power consumption is not clear,
since, as we have already seen, the difference of the power consumption of Xeon
Phi and Skylake Xeon is rather small even though the integer cores are completely
different.

The latencies of the floating point units of Skylake and A64fx are quite different.
The same is true for the latency of L1 and L2 data caches. The latency of FMA
operation of Skylake is four, while that of A64fx is nine (See Table 4.3). The

Table 4.3 Latencies of
Instructions

	Skylake	A64fx
FMA	4	9
Load (From L1D)	4-6	11
L2D Hit	14	37-47

extremely deep pipeline of A64fx probably made the use of slow and low-power transistors possible, and thus reduces the power consumption.

We can see that these Japanese processors are designed for the set of applications quite different from the set for which Intel processors are designed. The main memory bandwidth is higher, while the on-chip bandwidth between the cache hierarchy is smaller. As a result, the the energy efficiency is higher.

The primary target of these processors are applications which require relatively high memory bandwidth. For these applications relatively low L2D bandwidth is not a serious problem. Among the application categories we discussed in Chap. 3, both structured and unstructured mesh share this characteristics. Strictly speaking, as we have discussed in Sect. 3.1, structured mesh calculations can be efficiently executed on architectures with high cache memory bandwidth and low main memory bandwidth [11]. However, to achieve high efficiency for structured mesh calculation using cache requires a complete reorganization of the loop and data structure, and on machines with low LLC bandwidth it is difficult to improve the efficiency. Thus A64fx and SX-Aurora show one unique kind of co-evolution of software and hardware, where the processor architecture is optimized to existing software and the software is optimized to existing processor architecture. This approach can and probably does find the local optimal point in the design space, but whether or not that is the global optimum or not is the question we should keep in our mind.

The number of transistors of one 48-core A64fx chip is 8.8×10^9, only slightly larger than that of the 28-core Intel Skylake Xeon processor. They both have 16 floating-point units per core. Thus, we can say that A64fx uses 40% less transistors per floating-point unit. Thus, A64fx falls between Skylake and Knights Landing for the transistor efficiency.

The energy efficiency of A64fx is quite impressive. The measured performance per watt of the entire system for HPL is 15.418 GF/W, while the best number for Skylake Xeon is 5.843 GF/W [12]. Since the technologies used are different, we cannot directly compare the efficiencies of these processors. However, as we have already discussed the difference in the feature size makes relatively small difference in the power, and certainly this nearly a factor of three difference cannot be explained by the difference in the technologies only. Compared to Skylake, A64fx has significantly smaller amount of out-of-order resources, smaller L1 and L2 bandwidth, and larger latencies for arithmetic units and L1 and L2 data caches, all of them should have contributed to its much lower power consumption.

On the other hand, these differences made it much more difficult to achieve reasonable efficiencies for real applications on A64fx. Odajima et al. [13] analyzed the performance of a simple particle-particle interaction kernel on A64fx, and found that the combination of the large latency of the floating-point units and limited number of architecture registers resulted in relatively low efficiency. The number of architecture registers for the SVE units of A64fx is 32.

Listing 4.1 Simple interaction kernel

```
dx  = xi - xj;
dy  = yi - yj;
dz  = zi - zj;
r2  = dx*dx + dy*dy + dz*dz + e2;
r3i= pow(r2, -1.5);
ff  = mj*r3i;
fx  += ff*dx;
fy  += ff*dy;
fz  += ff*dz;
```

Consider a simple interaction kernel of 4.1. Here, xi, yi, zi are the three coordinates of the position $\mathbf{x}_i$ particle i, xj, yj, zj are those of particle j, mj is the mass of particle j and $e2$ is a constant used to prevent the divergence of force at $\mathbf{x}_i = \mathbf{x}_j$ (the softening parameter [14]). We loop over the index j to obtain the force on particle i.

Let us estimate the number of cycles necessary to complete one interaction calculation. We assume all operations have the same latency of u cycles, except the pow function, which consists of fast initial guess and Newton-Raphson iteration. For simplicity, we assume that the latency of the pow function is $5u$. The critical dependency path would be xj - dx - $(dx*dx+e2)$ - $(dx*dx+dy*dy+e2)$ - $(dx*dx+dy*dy+dz*dz+e2)$ - $r3i$ - ff - fx and thus the latency is $7u + 5u = 12u$. Thus, with the latency of 9 cycles, we need around 110 cycles from the start of the first iteration to the end of the interaction. The number of instructions per one interaction would be around 15. Thus, to achieve the near-peak performance, $15 \times 110 \times 2 = 330$ instructions should be issued before the first iteration is finished. Here the additional factor of two comes from the fact that A64fx has two SVE units. On the other hand, the number of renaming registers is only 96 [10]. Thus, if we just rely on the OoO execution, we can get roughly 1/3 of throughput of the arithmetic units for this simple kernel. Actual performance is even lower since there are other factors which further reduce the efficiency, such as the branch prediction penalty and the size of the instruction reorder buffer.

There are many ways to avoid this kind of inefficiencies, and the most widely used is the simultaneous multithreading (SMT). With SMT, a processor core runs multiple (typically two or four) independent threads. If there are two threads, they are executed in every alternating cycles. They do not share the registers. Thus, from software point of view, two threads looks like two processors running at the half clock speed, but with the same latency in the unit of clock cycles. Thus, the latency, viewed from threads, is one half of the hardware latency. It is therefore much easier to hide. A more straightforward approach would be to increase the number of architecture registers. This approach was adopted for the SPARC64 VIIIfx processor used for the K computer [15]. However, for the SVE instruction set, Fujitsu chose not to adopt this approach.

One additional advantage of the SMT approach is that the register file for an SMT processor is easier to design and thus more power efficient compared to the register file of similar size designed for a single-thread processor, since the register files for different threads are physically independent. Thus SMT approach has been adopted by most of modern processors.

Yet another way would be to design a vector processor, on which each operation takes multiple cycles.

The lesson here is that details of the instruction architecture and microarchitecture do matter. They do affect the power efficiency, and also the application efficiency, sometimes in unexpected ways in particular when there are additional constraints due to the instruction set architecture.

4.5 SIMD Supercomputers—Illiac IV and TMC CM-2

An obvious way to reduce the logic circuits not used to arithmetic units is to adopt the SIMD arithmetic unit, and microprocessors have followed this strategy in the last two decade. In the case of Intel x86 processors, SIMD units with width of 2, 4, 8 have been used with SSEx, AVX(2), and AVX512 instruction sets. This in-core SIMD approach is, however, not the only way to take advantage of an SIMD architecture, and in the past SIMD supercomputers with very large numbers of execution units were built. They include Illiac IV [16–18] and TMC CM-1 and CM-2 [19]. There are also other important machines such as Goodyear MPP [20], ICL DAP [21] and Maspar MP-1 and MP-2 [22]. However, they lacked the hardware support for floating-point operations and thus they are not the target of our analysis here. The primary target of both Illiac IV and CM-2 were large-scale simulations, and they were designed to achieve high floating-point throughput.

4.5.1 Illiac IV

Illiac IV consisted of 64 processing elements (PEs), and the clock frequency was 12.5 MHz. The peak floating point performance was 40–55 Mflops for double precision operations [18]. Thus, one floating-point operation took about 20 cycles. The total gate count of one PE is around 10,000. Unfortunately the meaning of "gates" here is not clear. Let us assume that it is the same as that of gates used in Cray-1, since both Illiac IV and Cray-1 were made using ECL gates. Therefore, we assume that the number of ECL gates necessary to construct the combinatorial logic part of a fully pipelined floating-point multiplier is 30 k. The total gate count of Illiac IV was 640 k, and it could perform 1.5 FMA operations per cycle, corresponding to the transistor efficiency of $30 \times 1.5/640 = 7.0\%$.

Thus, even though the multi-cycle floating-point arithmetic unit was adopted, the transistor efficiency of Illiac IV was very high, comparable to those of Cray-1 and Intel i860. Compared to the efficiency of 2.8% of CDC 6600, the transistor efficiency of Illiac IV is 2.5 times higher. Thus, at least these nominal transistor efficiency is concerned, the large-scale SIMD design pays off.

Whether the Illiac IV was successful or not is of course an entirely different question. Even though it played an important role as the research platform for parallel programming, there were no followup project, and the Illiac IV project was not regarded as a great success. The reason seems to be mostly the problems in the hardware development. The initial design, in which a 20-gate ECL IC chips and thin-film memory were used, turned out to be too ambitious, and the logic design was changed to use smaller IC chips, and the resulted increase in the physical circuit size made it impossible to use the thin-film memory. As a result, bipolar SRAM chips were adopted as the main memory, which was actually a very good move. However, the project was delayed by several years, the cost increased from 8M USD to 31 M USD, the design was shrunken from 256 PEs to 64 PEs, the clock frequency was reduced from 25 MHz to 12.5 MHz. Thus, compared to what was initially proposed, the system actually built was much more costly and yet slow.

We have seen that CDC 6600 had 100 K ECL-equivalent gates and Cray-1 had 230 K. Thus, even compared with Cray-1, which was completed several years after Illiac IV was completed, Illiac IV had three times more gates, and this large gate count resulted in the huge machine size and a low clock frequency. Illiac IV was 15 meters long, 3 meters tall, and 2.4 meters wide. Cray-1 has the diameter of 1.4 meters and the height of two meters. The clock frequency of Illiac IV was comparable to that of CDC 6600. If the original design goal had been achieved, it would be comparable to that of CDC 7600.

What we can learn from the design and history of Illiac IV are

- A large-scale SIMD design does offer the advantage in the transistor efficiency of a factor of two or three, even when compared with relatively transistor-efficient designs.
- The need to make the entire machine work on the single clock put the physical limit to the clock frequency.
- The use of the premature semiconductor technology kills projects.

4.5.2   CM-2

Even though Illiac IV and CM-2 fall to the same category of large-scale SIMD supercomputer, they are quite different in many aspects. First of all, CM-2 is physically much smaller. It is a cube of about 1.5 m on a side. Despite its small size, the number of processors and the number of floating-point units integrated in CM-2 is impressive. The complete CM-2 consisted of 65,536 1-bit processors. One processor chip houses 16 processors, and 4096 processor chips are connected to form a 12-dimensional hypercube. The floating-point operation capability was provided by the attached floating-point chip, Weitek 3164 (or 3132). Weitek 3164 could perform one multiplication and one addition in every clock period. It had a 32-word register file and one bidirectional I/O port. One Weitek chip was shared by two processor chips, resulting in total 2048 FMA units in one machine. CM-2 was up and running as of 1987, and certainly was the machine with by far the largest number of floating-point units at that time.

The measured highest performance of CM-2 was for 32-bit polynomial evaluation and that exceeded 20 Gflops. If we regard this number as the peak throughput of the Weitek chips, most likely their clock period was 5 MHz. For the matrix multiplication, the measured performance at that time was 5 Gflops. [23]. The total power consumption of CM-2 is 28 kW [23]. This was much lower than those of vector-parallel machines (both from Cray or Japanese vendors), which were in the range of 100–300 kW.

The total transistor count of Weitek 3164 is unknown, but most likely between 150 K and 200 k, with a fully pipelined 64-bit floating point unit and a 32×64 register file. The single CM processor chip contains 50 K transistors [19]. Thus, the total number of transistors per one floating point unit is less than 300 K. For the nominal number of 120 k transistors per floating-point unit, the transistor efficiency of CM-2 is 30%, an extremely large number.

One practical limitation of CM-2 is that the width of the data path between the Weitek and processor chips is 32 bits. Thus, the B/F number is only two, which was not sufficient to keep the floating-point unit busy for most of applications. For the matrix-matrix multiply, we can store 4×4 matrix in the register file. Thus, once that matrix is stored, we can load 4 words in 8 cycles, calculate matrix-vector multiplication in 16 cycles, and store the results in 8 cycles, Thus it is not impossible to achieve a near-peak performance for the matrix-matrix multiplication.

With the originally designed way to use the FP unit, this kind of the reduction of the necessary memory bandwidth was not possible, because the original model was that the 32 1-bit processors share one FP unit. For one floating-point operation, these 32 processors first send their operand in parallel, but for each processor one bit per cycle. The interface chip is placed between CM processor chips and Weitek chip, which performs the transpose operation for the 32 64-bit words, so that it can send 64-bit words to Weitek chip. Thus, 32 data are sent to the FP unit in 128 cycles. Then another 32 data is sent to the interface chip between the CM processor chip and the Weitek chip. This part can be done concurrently with the sending of the initial 32 words to the Weitek chip. Then in the next 64 cycles the data in the interface chip is sent to Weitek chip, and the operation is done. In the next 64 cycles the result is sent to the interface chip, and then in the final 64 cycles the calculated result is sent back to CM processor chips. Thus, the total procedure consists of 320 cycles. One could overlap the stages to send the data for the next operation with the execution stage and the data transfer from Weitek and interface chips, so that the number of cycles per operation is reduced from 10 to 6. If the calculation result is immediately used in the next operation and not used in later operations, the next operation requires only four cycles per operation. However, this would be very much the maximum throughput.

Later, TMC introduced a new programming model, in which the 32 processors connected to the Weitek chip are regarded as one 32-bit processor. In other words, one 32-bit word was stored horizontally over these 32 processors. In this way, there was no need for the transpose operation in the interface chip, and the register file in the Weitek chip could be used to store intermediate data. Thus, it should have become possible to achieve much higher performance for operations such as the matrix-matrix multiply.

In 1987, Cray Y-MP was under development. Cray X-MP/4 had just four arithmetic units. ETA-10 had 16, but its shared memory was not working. (The author was using ETA-10 at the John von Neumann Supercomputer Center in summer of 1987). The reason why CM-2 could integrate two-orders-of-magnitude more floating point arithmetic units was that CMOS VLSI circuits were used. In 1980s, The clock speed that could be achieved with CMOS was much lower than that possible with ECL circuits, but the gap was rapidly closing. In 1989, there were many single-chip floating-point arithmetic units with the clock period of up 33 MHz or higher, while the highest clock periods of vector supercomputer was 245 MHz of Cray-2.

The design of CM-2 clearly demonstrated the fact that an SIMD design can achieve extremely high transistor efficiency and at the same time reasonably high application efficiency.

4.5.3   Problems with Large-Scale SIMD Processors

Well, if the design of CM-2 was so good, why it was replaced with a more traditional vector-processor design in CM-5, and why the company eventually went bankrupt? In this section we discuss the limitations of large-scale SIMD architectures.

4.5.3.1   Synchronous System Clock

There are two clear architectural limitations in the design of all large-scale SIMD processors in 1980s and early 1990s. The first one is that one system, which is of the physical size of one to a few meters, was designed to operate synchronously on a single clock signal. Such a design was certainly possible when the clock frequency was low, such as 8 MHz of CM-2. However, by early 1990s, the clock frequency of CMOS single-chip microprocessors reached 100 MHz and higher. It was quite difficult to design a multi-PCB system with the system clock higher than 100 MHz, even with ECL technology. Cray-1 reached 80 MHz in 1976, but even in 1988 Cray Y-MP and NEC SX-3 had the clock of 167 MHz. Thus, it had become quite difficult to design a large-scale SIMD processor with the clock frequency comparable to that of single-chip microprocessors.

Many SIMD processors had two-dimensional grid network. For the grid network, the hardware and control logic can be very simple if we can assume that neighboring processors execute the exactly the same operation at the same clock cycle. For example, if all processors send the data to its left neighbor, they can all receive the data from their right neighbors at the next clock cycle. This simple communication logic is only possible when all processors operate on the single clock with a small skew. One could always add FIFO to the channels between processors which would take care of clock skews, but the increase in the gate count can be significant.

In the case of CM-2, the hypercube part of the network could perform complex routing, and thus the router logic probably had all necessary logics for packet routing. Therefore, there seems to be no reason to force all processor chips to operate on a single clock. As far as the clock source is the same, we can design a large-scale SIMD processors with large clock skews between processors. Thus, we suspect that the problem with the synchronous clock and interprocessor network could have been solved.

4.5.3.2   Memory Bandwidth

The second and more serious one is the problem of the memory bandwidth. The designs of Illiac IV and TMC CM-2 relied on the external semiconductor memory which were very fast compared to the speed of the processor. The cycle time of the SRAM memory of Illiac IV was 240 ns, while one floating-point operation on one PE of Illiac IV took more than one microsecond. With the even lower clock period of 8 MHz, CM-2 had a similarly high B/F number.

However, with the advance of the semiconductor technology, the amount of the gates we can integrate in a chip increased quickly. Moreover, the clock cycle of the logic within a chip also increased rapidly. On the other hand, the communication bandwidth to the external memory could not increase fast enough to keep up with the increases in the clock speed and gate count of the CMOS logic chips.

This problem was actually already there with the Weitek 3164 chip used in CM-2. The Weitek chip itself could operate with 16 MHz (and eventually 25 and 33 MHz) clock, but the low clock frequency of the CM-2 processor did not allow much improvement in the performance throughout the lifetime of CM-2, from 1986 to 1992. In the same 6 years, the clock period of single-chip microprocessors increased from around 20 MHz to 150 MHz. No large-scale SIMD processor with such a high clock frequency appeared. The MasPar MP-2, introduced in 1992, operated on the clock of 12.5 MHz [24]. We did not discuss MasPar systems because they lack the hardware support for floating-point operations. The peak single-precision floating-point performance of one MP-2 processor chip (32PEs) was around 10 Mflops.

Thus what happened in the history is that nobody had tried to design (or suc-ceeded in designing) a large-scale SIMD processor with the clock speed comparable to that of single-chip microprocessors, even though it would have been possible. However, if one would tried to design such a processor, the problem of limited memory bandwidth should be solved. In the case of single-chip microprocessors, as we have seen in Sect. 4.3, this problem was "solved" by adding a deep hierarchy of cache memories. As we have already seen, this resulted in the tremendous loss in the efficiency, both for the transistor or power efficiency and the application efficiency. Even so, at least in early 1990s, systems based on single-chip microprocessors outperformed both vector processors and large-scale SIMD processors.

A natural question would be the following. Couldn't we make use of some memory hierarchy to reduce the B/F requirement of SIMD or vector processors?

One might think the answer is no, and in early 1990s people certainly thought so. As far as the use of the cache hierarchy is concerned, this answer is probably right. Consider a large-scale SIMD processor. If we add a cache memory to each PE, we can imagine that for every load instruction, even if the cache hit rate is very high, there may be one or more PEs which experience the cache miss. Since we have an SIMD system, with one cache miss in any PE all PEs must stall. Thus, even with cache, a large-scale SIMD processor would stall at every load operation.

In the case of vector-parallel processors, in principle the penalty of the cache miss is much smaller than that for large-scale SIMD processors, since they are MIMD systems. When one processor experience the cache miss, that processor woulds stall. However, other processors can proceed, up to the point where they communicate with each other. Thus, if the interval of communication is long enough, we can expect that on average all processors would experience a similar number of cache miss, and thus would not be slowed down by the stalling of other processors.

The reason why the cache memory was (at least in early 1990s) not effective is the way the application sofware was written. The applications optimized for vector processors in 1970s and 1980s had the loops over large arrays, since it is the way to extract the best performance from vector processors with sufficient memory bandwidth.

On the other hand, for such programs, cache memory would not help much, since for each simple loops, the memory area accessed is much bigger than the cache size. If we divide the loops so that one loop would fit into the cache and change the program structure, in principle we can improve the performance.

Listing 4.2 Program with simple long loops

```
for(i=0;i<n;i++){
  for(j=0;j<n;j++){
    a[i][j] = 2*b[i][j]-(b[i][j-1]+b[i][j+1]);
  }
}
for(i=0;i<n;i++){
  for(j=0;j<n;j++){
    c[i][j] = 2*a[i][j]-(a[i][j-1]+a[i][j+1]);
  }
}
```

Listing 4.2 illustrates a program suitable for vector processors. We ignore the handling of boundary values for simplicity. We have two double loops, and the first one loops over a and b, and the second one over a and c. If we do not use a in the rest of the program, we could rewrite these loops as in Listing 4.3.

Listing 4.3 Program with merged loops

```
for(i=0;i<n;i++){
   for(j=0;j<n;j++){
      a[j] = 2*b[i][j]-(b[i][j-1]+b[i][j+1]);
   }
   for(j=0;j<n;j++){
      c[i][j] = 2*a[j]-(a[j-1]+a[j+1]);
   }
}
```

However, on vector machines this rewrite might not improve the performance, Actually, in this simple example it might do, but for real application codes with many operations, the innermost loop might become too complex and too long to be analyzed by compilers, and they might fail in vectorizing the code. Also, programs with simple loops are much easier to understand and debug.

We should note that this problem is the problem of the language construct and the way the application program written in a language is compiled into the machine code. Since the loop in Listing 4.2 can be regarded as a parallel operation on all elements of arrays, in principle compilers can generate whatever instruction sequences it wants to generate as long as the result is correct.

4.6 GPGPUs

GPGPUs have the architecture rather similar to large-scale SIMD machines we have just discussed, but with cache memories. Thus, it is important to understand how GPGPUs solved the two problems of large-scale SIMD processors, the clock frequency and the memory bandwidth.

The essential idea of solution for NVIDIA GPGPUs is to limit the unit of SIMD execution to relatively small units which they named SM (Streaming Multiprocessor). Each SM consists of a relatively small number of what they call Cuda cores, which is a processing element. In the case of the A100 GPU [25], one chip contains 108 SMs. Each SM contains 64 FP32 Cuda cores. Thus, the total number of Cuda core is 6912. Each SM also contains four Tensor Cores.

One Tensor Core of A100 can perform 256 FP16 FMA operations per clock. Therefore, the total number of FP16 FMA units in one chip is $256 \times 4 \times 108 = 110{,}592$. The peak performance is 312Tflops, and this means the clock frequency is 1.4 GHz. The peak performance for usual FP32 operation is 19.5 Tflops, also consistent with the clock frequency of 1.4 GHz. Each of 64 Cuda cores in one SM is able to perform one FP32 FMA per cycle.

The number of SIMD cores sounds large, but compared to the number of FP units per core of modern microprocessors such as Intel Skylake Xeon and Fujitsu

A64fx, actually they are not much different. One AVX512 unit contains 16 FP32 FMA units, and there are two AVX512 units per core. Thus one Skylake core has 32 FP32 FMA units. With a large number of relatively small SM units in one chip, the performance penalty of the cache miss of one Cuda core can be made much smaller compared to the case of a chip-scale SIMD processor.

Another important architectural characteristics of NVIDIA GPUs is their huge register files. The size of the register file for one SM is 256 KB. (The same for two previous generations, NVIDIA P100 and V100). This means register files of 4 KB, or 1024 32-bit words, per FP32 core. The size of the register file is larger than that of the L1 cache, and even larger than that of L2 cache for the case of P100 and V100. Thus the roles of "registers" and cache memories are completely different from those for microprocessors. Conceptually, the largest on-chip storage of NVIDIA GPGPUs is the register file. Thus, any reusable data should be kept on the register files, not in L1 or L2 caches. The hardware and software support for a large number of threads makes it possible to use registers as primary storage of reused data, though not necessarily in the best possible way. The approach used to hide the latency of the main memory is to use a large number of threads per Cuda core. For this purpose, the register file is divided to smaller units, each of which is accessed from one thread. The usual way to use this multithread feature is to run the same kernel. Thus, even though the idea is multithreading, each processor behaves as vector processors. Thus, we can allow large latency for the main memory access, as long as the memory access is not too frequent.

Since the largest data storage is close to arithmetic units, the data movement within the chip is minimized, contributing to high performance per watt. Also, the support of hardware multithreading makes the design of large register files easy and energy- and area-efficient (no need to multi-ported memory).

One important feature of the cache memory of NVIDIA GPGPUs is that the coherency management is removed. As a result, its cache memory is relatively power-efficient. Of course, this means that the application programs should takes care of the coherency whenever necessary. This is inconvenient but not impossible.

NVIDIA GPUs clearly show that medium-scale (64 cores) SIMD architecture works well, at least for applications for which GPUs worked well, such as structured mesh, particles, and dense matrices. Right now, the main market of GPUs is the deep learning, where the dense matrix-matrix multiplication dominates the calculation. Thus, two latest generations of NVIDIA GPUs have specialized arithmetic units for matrix-matrix multiplication. The V100 has logic for 4×4 matrix-matrix multiplication in FP16 format. With A100, matrix multiplication is supported also for FP64. Whether or not such architecture is useful for applications other than deep learning remains to be seen, but it makes sense from the viewpoint of hardware vendor. If what most of customer wants is the performance of matrix-matrix multiplication, specialized logic is clearly the best solution.

The total number of transistors on one A100 chip is 5.42×10^{10} [25], while the number of FP64 FMA units is 6912. Thus, the number of transistors per one FMA unit is 7.84×10^6. To obtain the transistor efficiency we should divide the standard number of 130 k transistors per FMA unit by the above number, and the answer is 1.66%. Surprizingly, the transistor efficiency of A100 is lower than that of Intel Xeon Phi and only slightly higher than that of Fujitsu A64fx. The total transistor count for register files and L1 and L2 cache memories is not very large, since there are only around 100 MB of memory cells. Apparently, most of transistors on the A100 die are used for something other than the on-chip memory or floating-point arithmetic units.

4.7 PEZY Processors and Sunway SW26010

4.7.1 PEZY Processors

The ExaScaler system based on the PEZY-SC processor was ranked #2 in the Green500 list of November 2014, with the measured performance of 4.95 Gflops/W. The number 1 score was 5.27 Gflops/W for a machine based on AMD FirePro S9150 and the number 3 was 4.45 for a machine based on NVIDIA K20x. The PEZY-SC is a 1024-core, MIMD massively parallel processor on chip. It is fabricated with TSMC 28 nm process and has the die size of around 400 mm^2. Each core has one FP64 FMA unit, and can run eight threads simultaneously. The second-generation PEZY-SC2 is very similar to PEZY-SC except that the number of core is doubled to 2048 and is fabricated with TSMC 16FF+ process. Here we overview the architecture of SC2.

One PE has a register file of size 2 KB, L1D and L1I caches of 2 and 4 KB, and the local storage of size 20 KB. Here, the local storage is the memory local to PE and with separate address space from the main memory. The 2048 PEs are organized in three levels of hierarchy. First, 16 PEs form one "city", with L2I and L2D caches of the sizes of 32 and 64 KB. Then 16 "cities" form a "prefecture", which has two L3 cache units, each with the size of 2560 KB. Finally, eight "prefectures" form one chip. Two prefectures share one DDR4 DRAM unit with the bandwidth of 25 GB/s. Thus, the L3 cache and the local memory both has the total capacity of 40 MB. L1 and L2 caches are much smaller.

As in the case of GPGPUs, the caches of PEZY-SCx are non-coherent. The information of the update of cache memory of one PE (or city or prefecture) is not transmitted to other PEs automatically. PEs need to execute the cash flash instruction to write back the data, and SCx support the flash operation to each level of the cache hierarchy. The line sizes of the L1, L2, and L3 data caches of the SC processor are 64, 256, and 1024 bytes [26]. By changing the line size, the designers of the PEZY-SC processor kept the bandwidth of L2 and L3 data caches very high. The bandwidth of L2D cache is the same as that for L1D, and L3D offers around half of them.

With the die size of 620 mm^2, the total transistor count of SC2 chip should be around 10^{10}. Thus, the number of transistors per FMA unit is 5×10^6, and the transistor efficiency is 2.4%. Thus, even though PEZY-SCx are fully MIMD processor without SIMD units within cores, it is more transistor-efficient than almost any other modern high-performance processor, including even GPGPUs or Intel Xeon Phi, both with wide SIMD execution units.

This quite high transistor efficiency was achieved by making the design of one PE very simple. It is a simple in-order core. However, with eight threads, there is not much need for instruction scheduling or register renaming. Thus, even though the core is simple, it is in practice highly efficient for many real applications.

The fact that one PE is simple and small apparently helped PEZY-SC processor to achieve very high power efficiency as well. The absence of the cache coherency should have helped a lot. Systems based on PEZY-SC and SC2 processors were listed #1 in the Green500 list for June and November of 2015, June 2016, November 2017, and June and November 2018.

In 2017, the development of SC3 was halted because Saito, the CEO of PEZY Computing, was arrested on suspicion of defrauding a government institution 4M USD. It is unfortunate that the development of PEZY processors has been halted for non-technical reasons. PEZY processors represent one approach to achieve very high transistor- and power-efficiencies with a clever MIMD design.

There was a plan to add very fast DRAM chips to SC2 processor, but the development was also halted for the same reason as that for SC3.

The effective memory bandwidth of the SC chip with eight channels of DDR3 memory is around 75 GB/s [26]. The theoretical peak performance of one SC chip, with the clock frequency of 733 MHz is 1.47 Tflops. Thus we have BF=0.05 for the SC processor. The B/F of SC2 is somewhat lower, since the number of memory channels was decreased from eight to four.

The programming environment of SCx processors is PZCL, a subset of OpenCL [27]. Both SC and SC2 are used as attached accelerator connected to the host through PCIe interface. The SC2 design included six MIPS64 cores, which can in principle run their own operating system, but existing systems all use Intel Xeon-D processors as the host computer.

4.7.2   Sunway SW26010

SW26010 is the CPU used for the Sunway Taihulight system [28, 29], which was listed #1 in the Top500 list from June 2016 to November 2017.

The TaihuLight system consists of 40,960 nodes, connected by the network with injection bandwidth of 8 GB/s per node.

The processor itself consists of four CGs (core groups), each with one MPE (management processing element) and 64 CPEs (computing processing elements). Both MPE and CPE are 64-bit RISC cores. MPE has L1 cache memories for both instructions and data, and also L2 data cache. On the other hand, each CPE has L1 instruction cache and 64 KB of local data memory. CPEs can communicate with the main memory through DMA as well as load/store instructions. Each CPE can initiate multiple asynchronous DMA operations. Thus, it is possible to write the kernel loop so that the computation, DMA read for the data which will be necessary for the next iteration, and DMA write operation of the result of the previous iteration all run concurrently and thus the communication with the main memory is completely hidden. This capability of explicit control of communication with main memory is crucial for achieving high efficiency.

Each core group is connected to 8 GB DDR3 DRAM with the theoretical peak transfer rate of 41 GB/s. The processor runs at the clock frequency of 1.45 GHz, and each core (both MPE and CPE) can perform four double precision FMA operations. Thus, the theoretical peak performance of one processor is 3060 Gflops and that of one CG is 765 Gflops. Here again, BF=0.05.

CPEs in one CG are organized into an 8 × 8 array, and within each row or column, low-latency, high-bandwidth point-to-point and broadcast communications are supported. This network allows broadcast and reduction over CPEs with very low overhead and thus make fine-grained parallelism possible on CPE, even though they are running in an MIMD fashion.

Operating system runs on MPE, and by default the user program also runs on MPE. In order to use CPEs, there are two ways. One is to use an extension of OpenACC [30] designed for the SW26010 processor, and the other is use a lightweight thread library called Athread. Athread is more difficult to use compared to OpenACC, but allows fine-grained control of CPEs.

Because of its heterogeneous structure, one might imagine that SW26010 is similar to systems with GPGPUs. However, there are several important differences between systems with GPGPUs and SW26010. The largest one which makes the strategy for program development completely different is the fact that, even though the code on the CPE side should use DMA, the memory bandwidth of CPEs combined is much higher than that of MPE. This is true not only for continuous access but also for random access.

In the case of GPGPU, there is the communication bottleneck between CPU memory and GPU memory, and thus we need to carefully design the algorithm so that the communication between CPU and GPU is minimized. In the case of the SW26010 processor, using CPEs to access main memory access is actually faster than using MPE. Thus, almost any operation is actually faster on CPEs than on MPE, at least when implemented carefully using Athread and asynchronous DMA operations.

Since the data move between the main memory and CPE is faster than that between MPE and main memory, the strategy for program optimization for SW26010 is quite different from that for GPGPU and actually much closer to that for traditional vector processors. Almost any loop which is reasonably long can get benefit from moving to CPE. Of course, since the memory bandwidth of CPEs is very small compared to their floating-point arithmetic performance, we then need to write the kernel code so that it does as many calculations as possible for one memory access.

Thus, as in the case of vector processors, the performance optimization on SW26010 can be done in a step-by-step, one-loop-at-a-time way. This means the debugging is relatively easy and thus development cycle is actually pretty fast.

One problem of current software tools for SW26010 is that the optimization capability of the compiler for CPE is rather limited. Thus, in order to achieve the efficiency close to the theoretical peak performance for the inner kernels, it is currently necessary to manually schedule instructions through writing the innermost kernel in assembly language.

Unfortunately, nothing is known about the die size, technology used or transistor count of SW26010. However, even if we assume that it is fabricated using the most advanced technology such as TSMC 16FF, the measured performance per watt of 6.051 Gflops/W was quite impressive. In fact, the system was listed # 4 in the November 2016 Green500 list. NVIDIA P100 took # 1 and 2, and PEZY-SC #3. NVIDIA P100 was made with TSMC's 16FF+ technology.

One of Chinese exascale systems will be based on the successor of SW26010, with SIMD width and the number of core groups both doubled [31]. To reach exaflops, they will need to double the number of processor chips as well.

4.8   Conclusion

In this chapter, we have overviewed representative HPC systems and microprocessors, starting from CDC 6600 and up to systems in 2020 such as Intel Skylake Xeon, NVIDIA A100, Fujitsu Z64fx, NEC SX-Aurora, PEZY SC2, and Sunway TaihuLight, from the viewpoints of transistor- and power-efficiency. Since the actual performance-per-watt numbers depends on the semiconductor technology used, here we focus on the transistor efficiency, which we found to be closely related to the power efficiency.

Table 4.4 lists the processors which we discussed in this chapter. For Intel processors, we list only four, the first i860, and the latest Skylake, and two which lie near the bottom of the efficiency.

Table 4.4   The architectural features of processors discussed

	Single Core	MIMD	In core SIMD	Global SIMD	Coherent Cache	Non-Coherent Cache	Local memory	Transistor efficiency
CM-2	–	–	–	✓	–	–	✓	30%
Illiac IV	–	–	–	✓	–	–	✓	7%
Cray-1	✓	–	–	–	–	–	–	6.5%
Intel i860	✓	–	–	–	–	✓	–	6.5%
PEZY-SC	–	✓	–	–	–	✓	✓	2.4%
NVIDIA A100	–	✓	–	✓	–	✓	✓	1.7%
Fujitsu A64fx	–	✓	✓	–	✓	–	–	1.3%
Intel Skylake	–	✓	✓	–	✓	–	–	0.8%
Intel P4	✓	–	✓	–	–	✓	–	0.3%
Intel Core2	–	✓	✓	–	✓	–	–	0.08%
Sunway SW26010	–	✓	✓	–	–	–	✓	–

What we can see from this list is that an architecture with global SIMD and local memory gives the best transistor efficiency. The transistor efficiency of Illiac IV is not very high, but that is due to the non-pipelined design of the arithmetic units. As we have seen in Sect. 4.1, a fully pipelined design would be around three times more transistor efficient, and that means the real fraction of the gates used for arithmetic units is around 20%. Thus, global SIMD design with local memory can improve the transistor efficiency by an order of magnitude over modern processors.

It should be noted that this comparison, in particular that for CM-2 and Illiac IV is somewhat unfair, since the transistor count of these two processors does not include the transistor count for on-chip memories. They did not have cache and the only memory unit is the external main memory. On the other hand, one could argue that if more than half of the total transistors on chip is used for on-chip memories, that design is not really optimal and there must be some way to improve the efficiency. Therefore, we argue that, even though the efficiency number of 30% might be an overestimate, our goal should not be too far from that when we take into account the contribution of on-chip memories, and if we only count the transistors for the CPU core without including cache or local memory, 30% is a feasible goal.

Of course, a high nominal transistor efficiency itself is not useful if the application efficiency is low. However, experiences with Illiac IV and CM-2 actually have shown that these machines can achieve high efficiency for a wide variety of applications. The main reason why the global SIMD machines have disappeared in early 1990s is that it seemed there were no way to implement something like cache for a global SIMD processor.

To some extent, this problem was solved with NVIDIA GPGPUs, by making the unit of SIMD execution small. However, even though the SIMD architecture is used, the transistor efficiency of NVIDIA GPUs is not much higher than that of MIMD manycore processors. Thus, if our goal is the transistor efficiency of a few percents, both of small-scale SIMD processors and fully MIMD processors would work perfectly. If we want to achieve a higher efficiency, we need a different approach.

Though an MIMD architecture is adopted, SW 26010 represents an alternative approach: processors without cache and with local memory. Historically, similar approach had been adopted in several designs, such as CDC 7600, Cray-2, Sony/IBM Cell BE/PowerXCell [32], and NVIDIA G80/G90/GTX200. Well, we can see that this local memory architecture has been adopted several times but have not survived to present day. The main problem with the local memory was that the performance improvement is neither automatic not portable. In the case of CDC 7600, its successor, Cray-1, had the main memory bandwidth large enough so that the local memory was not necessary. Interestingly, Seymour Cray chose to revive the local memory with Cray-2 and also with Cray-3 [33]. The development of Cray-3 started around 1985. Unfortunately, the development of Cray-3 was delayed for many years and the Company, Cray Computer Corporation, filed for bankruptcy on March 1995. The main reason of the delay was the use of the GaAs device, which also caused serious problems during the development of Numerical Wind Tunnel [34] and its commercial version, Fujitsu VPP500, a few years later. Cray-2 was not a great commercial success. The reason is that it had to compete with Cray X-MP, which offered performance similar to that of Cray-2 and much higher software compatibility to Cray-1 a few years earlier than Cray-2. The design with the local memory is not the unique cause of the failure, but certainly made the machine less popular.

Sony/IBM Cell processor was used in Sony PlayStation/3 and thus a huge number was made, but its use for systems other than PS/3 did not grow as expected. The Cell processor for PS/3 did not support double-precision arithmetic. It supported single-precision arithmetic, with the rounding toward zero [32]. The double-precision performance was not very high. Thus it was not easy to use the Cell processor for Scientific computing. Later, IBM developed a design with improved support for the double precision arithmetic, PowerXCell 8i, which appeared in 2008 with the theoretical peak performance of 108.8 Gflops. At that time, AMD was shipping 4-core "Barcelona" Opteron with the theoretical peak performance of 40Gflops. Also, NVIDIA GTX280 was announced in 2008, with the double-precision peak performance of 78Gflops and single-precision performance of 933 Gflops. Thus, the advantage of the PowerXCell processor was not very large.

NVIDIA GPUs up to this GTX280 also had local memory architecture. With Fermi, NVIDIA moved from the local memory architecture to cache-based architecture. This move certainly made the programming of GPGPUs easier, or at least looking easier. As we have already seen, since the coherency is not supported by hardware, the transistor- and power-efficiency of NVIDIA GPGPUs with cache has been fairly high, resulting in the processors with the highest peak performance, top-level performance per watt, and highly competitive pricing.

Thus, for the design of the commercial product, the choice of NVIDIA and PEZY to have relatively fine-grained MIMD processor with non-coherent cache seems to pay off, as far as they can offer the best products in the market. On the other hand, as we have seen in this chapter, such architectures are not optimal. In the next chapter, we discuss modern manycore designs which are close to the theoretical optimal, at least for the transistor- and power efficiency. We also discuss the application efficiency of those designs.

References

1. J.E. Thornton, *Design of a computer The Control Data 6600* (Scott, Foresman and Company, Glenvew, 1970)
2. J.S. Kolodzey, IEEE Trans. Compon. Hybrids Manuf. Technol. **4**(2), 181 (1981)
3. Cray Research, Inc., *The Cray-2 Computer System* (1985)
4. N. Marguls, Byte **14**(12), 333+ (1989)
5. L. Kohn, N. Marguls, IEEE MICRO **9**(July/August), 15 (1989)
6. D. Perlmutter, M. Kagan, The $i860^{tm}$ second generation of the $i860^{tm}$ supercomputing microprocessor family. Presentation given in Hot Chips 3, August 26–27, 1991. Stanford, USA (1991). https://old.hotchips.org/archives/1990s/hc03/

7. Intel Corporation. Intel® 64 and ia-32 architectures optimization reference manual (2020). Order Number: 248966-043

8. S. Yamamura, T. Aoki, H. Ando, Reserach Report of Information Processing Society of Japan. ARC **174**, 61 (2007). https://ci.nii.ac.jp/naid/110006420485/

9. Y. Yamada, S. Momose, Vector engine processor of nec's brand-new supercomputer sx-aurora tsubasa. Hot Chips **30**, 19–21 (2018)

10. Fujitsu Limited, A64fx® Microarchitecture Manual, rev 1.3 (2020). https://github.com/fujitsu/A64FX/blob/master/doc/A64FX_Microarchitecture_Manual_jp_1.3.pdf

11. H. Tanaka, Y. Ishihara, R. Sakamoto, T. Nakamura, Y. Kimura, K. Nitadori, M. Tsubouchi, J. Makino, in *Proceedings of the 2018 IEEE/ACM 4th International Workshop on Extreme Scale Programming Models and Middleware (ESPM2)* (2018), pp. 29–36

12. November 2020. https://www.top500.org/lists/green500/2020/11/

13. T. Odajima, Y. Kodama, M. Sato, in *Proceedings of the 2018 IEEE Symposium in Low-Power and High-Speed Chips (COOL CHIPS)* (2018), pp. 1–3. https://doi.org/10.1109/CoolChips.2018.8373083

14. S. J. Aarseth, Mon. Not. R. Astron. Soc. **126**, 223 (1963)

15. T. Maruyama, T. Yoshida, R. Kan, I. Yamazaki, S. Yamamura, N. Takahashi, M. Hondou, H. Okano, IEEE Micro **30**(2), 30 (2010)

16. G.H. Barnes, R.M. Brown, M. Kato, D.J. Kuck, D.L. Slotnick, R.A. Stokes, IEEE Trans. Comput. **C-17**(8), 746 (1968). https://doi.org/10.1109/TC.1968.229158

17. R.M. Hord, *The Illiac-IV: The first Supercomputer* (Computer Science, New York, 1982)

18. R.M. Hord, *Parallel Supercomputing in SIMD Architecture* (CRC Press, Boca Raton, 1990)

19. W.D. Hillis, *The Connection Machine* (MIT Press, Cambridge, 1985)

20. J.L. Potter, *The Massively Parallel Processor* (The MIT Press, Cambridge, 1985)

21. S.F. Reddaway, in *Proceedings of the 1st Annual Symposium on Computer Architecture* (ACM, Gainesville, 1973), pp. 61–65

22. T. Blank, in *Proceedings of the 35th IEEE Computer Society International Conference* (1990), pp. 25–28

23. L.W. Tucker, G.G. Robertson, IEEE Comput. **21**(8), 26 (1988)

24. Colsa Corp., The ground based rader digital hardware architecture implementation annual report (1993). https://apps.dtic.mil/dtic/tr/fulltext/u2/a263219.pdf

25. NVIDIA Corporation, Nvidia a100 tensor core GPU architecture (2020). https://www.nvidia.com/content/dam/en-zz/Solutions/Data-Center/nvidia-ampere-architecture-whitepaper.pdf

26. N. Yoshifuji, R. Sakamoto, K. Nitadori, J. Makino, in *Proceedings of the 2016 6th Workshop on Irregular Applications: Architecture and Algorithms (IA3)* (2016), pp. 58–61. https://doi.org/10.1109/IA3.2016.015

27. Khronos® OpenCL Working Group. The OpenCL™ Specification (2020). https://www.khronos.org/registry/OpenCL/specs/3.0-unified/html/OpenCL_API.html

28. H. Fu, J. Liao, J. Yang, L. Wang, Z. Song, X. Huang, C. Yang, W. Xue, F. Liu, F. Qiao, W. Zhao, X. Yin, C. Hou, C. Zhang, W. Ge, J. Zhang, Y. Wang, C. Zhou, G. Yang, Sci. China Inf. Sci. **59**(7), 072001 (2016). https://doi.org/10.1007/s11432-016-5588-7

29. J. Dongarra, Report on the sunway taihulight system (2016). http://www.netlib.org/utk/people/JackDongarra/PAPERS/sunway-report-2016.pdf

30. OpenACC-Standard.org, The openacc® application programming interface (2020). https://www.openacc.org/sites/default/files/inline-images/Specification/OpenACC-3.1-final.pdf

31. J. Gao, F. Zheng, F. Qi, Y. Ding, H. Li, H. Lu, W. He, H. Wei, L. Jin, X. Liu, D. Gong, F. Wang, Y. Zheng, H. Sun, Z. Zhou, Y. Liu, H. You, Sci. China Inf. Sci. **64**(4), 141101 (2021). https://doi.org/10.1007/s11432-020-3104-7

32. A. Arevalo, R.M. Matinata, M. Pandian, E. Peri, K. Ruby, F. Thomas, C. Almond, Programming the cell broadband engine™ architecture examples and best practices (2008). http://www.redbooks.ibm.com/redbooks/pdfs/sg247575.pdf

33. Cray Computer Corporation, The cray-2 computer system (1993)

34. H. Miyoshi, M. Fukuda, T. Iwamiya, T. Takamura, M. Tuchiya, M. Yoshida, K. Yamamoto, Y. Yamamoto, S. Ogawa, Y. Matsuo, T. Yamane, M. Takamura, M. Ikeda, S. Okada,

Y. Sakamoto, T. Kitamura, H. Hatama, M. Kishimoto, in *Supercomputing '94:Proceedings of the 1994 ACM/IEEE Conference on Supercomputing* (1994), pp. 685–692. https://doi.org/10.1109/SUPERC.1994.344334

Chapter 5
"Near-Optimal" Designs

Anyone can build a fast CPU. The trick is to build a fast system.

— Seymour Cray

In Chap. 4, we discussed the transistor- and power-efficiencies of general-purpose HPC processors, from CDC 6600 to modern processors such as Intel Skylake Xeon, Fujitsu A64fx, NEC SX-Aurora, PEZY-SC and SC2, NVIDIA A100, and Sunway SW26010. We have observed that the transistor efficiency varies widely, even among the modern processors, and correlate fairly well with the power efficiency.

In this chapter, we discuss more extreme designs. We start with our GRAPE-4 [1] and GRAPE-6 [2] processors, which are specialized to gravitational many-body simulations. They can be regarded as an idealized pipelined processors for particle-based simulations. Then we proceed to GRAPE-DR [3, 4], an chip-scale SIMD processor, and MN-Core, an SIMD processor optimized to deep learning. Finally, we discuss what additional functionalities we need to add to widen the application area of these processors.

5.1 The Special-Purpose Designs: GRAPE Processors

We started our GRAPE (GRAvity PipE) project [5] in 1988. The goal of the GRAPE project was to develop special-purpose processors for astrophysical N-body simulations. The astrophysical N-body problem is expressed as

$$\frac{d^2\mathbf{x}_i}{dt^2} = -\sum_j Gm_j \frac{\mathbf{x}_i - \mathbf{x}_j}{|\mathbf{x}_i - \mathbf{x}_j|^3}, \tag{5.1}$$

where $\mathbf{x}_i$ is the three-dimensional position vector of particle i, m_j is the mass of particle j, G is the gravitational constant and t is the time. This equation describes the motions of astronomical objects such as planets in our solar system, stars and dark matter in galaxies, and galaxies in the universe. Thus, it has a wide range

© Springer Nature Switzerland AG 2021
J. Makino, *Principles of High-Performance Processor Design*,
https://doi.org/10.1007/978-3-030-76871-3_5

of applications. Except for very small number of particles, the calculation cost of the right-hand side of Eq. 5.1 dominates the total cost, even when $O(N \log N)$ tree algorithm [6, 7] or $O(N)$ FMM [8, 9] are used. Thus, a special-purpose processor pays off. The basic approach of GRAPE project was to develop a fully pipelined processor to evaluate the right hand side of Eq. 5.1.

The GRAPE project started with GRAPE-1 [10], where the pipelined processor was constructed using general-purpose CMOS ICs, EPROMs and 16-bit adders. Several different word formats were used in GRAPE-1 pipeline. The position vectors were expressed in 16-bit fixed-point format. After the subtraction, the result was converted to eight-bit logarithmic format, with three bits used for fractional part. The final reduction of the calculated interaction was done on 48-bit fixed-point format. In this way, we could use 512k-bit and 1M-bit EPROMs for most of operations. The very short fractional part of GRAPE-1 of course limited the application range, but for galactic dynamics it gave reliable answer, as our error analysis have shown [11].

GRAPE-2 [12] was constructed using single-chip floating-point arithmetic chips such as Analog Devices 3201/3202 and TI SN74ACT8847. The position vectors were expressed in 64-bit floating-point format. After the initial position subtraction, the result was converted to 32-bit format, and all calculations before the final accumulation were done in this format. Even for problems which require high accuracy, it turned out to be sufficient to perform all calculations except the first position subtraction and the final accumulation in 32-bit format. To make the hardware small, the GRAPE-2 pipeline processed the three components of positions sequentially and calculated one interaction in every three clock cycles. The clock cycle was 4 MHz and its performance, if we count one interaction calculation as 30 floating-point operations, is 40 Mflops. In 1990, 40 Mflops was very fast for a machine of the cost of 2M JYE.

GRAPE-3 [13] was our first system with a custom-design ASIC processor chip. In early 1990s, the initial cost of ASIC was of the order of 100K USD. The GRAPE-3 processor design was essentially a custom-chip version of GRAPE-1. The main difference was that large EPROMs could not be used and thus operations in logarithmic format such as addition were implemented by fixed-point adders and small lookup tables. Figure 5.1 shows the mask pattern of the GRAPE-3 chip. It shows the pipeline structure of the processor chip rather well. The four big blocks in the bottom of the chip are the shifters and accumulators, and on the top half of the chip, the data flow is from left to right. The chip was designed using the module generator from Silicon Compiler Systems and thus was not a gate array design.

The total number of transistors of one GRAPE-3 processor chip was 110k, and it effectively performed 30 floating-point operations per cycle. If we interpret these 30 operations as 15 FMA operations, the number of transistors per FMA operation of GRAPE-3 processor chip was 7k, about 1/16 of the actual number necessary. This is of course due to the very short word format used and thus is not a fair comparison, but from the point of view of the applications, if the reduced accuracy is physically acceptable, GRAPE-3 can be used, and thus the best possible transistor- and power-

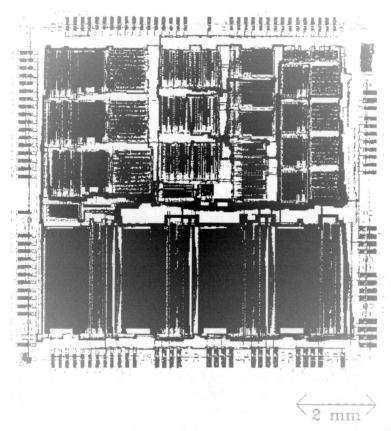

$\overleftarrow{2\ mm}\overrightarrow{}$

Fig. 5.1 The mask pattern of the GRAPE-3 chip

efficiency of a processor for a given application should depend on the accuracy required for each operation.

Many of modern processor support IEEE-754-2008 FP16 (binary16) format, which in principle can be used for some of operations for the interaction calculation. Unfortunately, experiments have shown that the gain is usually small, because of the overhead of converting the format is rather high. Another problem is that the exponent of FP16 format has only five bits, which is not sufficient to cover the dynamic range of many of astrophysical applications. The support of BF16 format with seven-bit exponent will certainly solve this problem, but the first problem of the overhead of conversion will be still there.

With GRAPE-4, we implemented the force calculation pipeline with the accuracy similar to that of the combination of FP64 and FP32. What is calculated using GRAPE-4 pipeline is the following two terms.

$$\mathbf{a}_i = \sum_j Gm_j \frac{\mathbf{r}_{ij}}{(r_{ij}^2 + \epsilon^2)^{3/2}} \tag{5.2}$$

$$\dot{\mathbf{a}}_i = \sum_j Gm_j \left[\frac{\mathbf{v}_{ij}}{(r_{ij}^2 + \epsilon^2)^{3/2}} - \frac{3(\mathbf{v}_{ij} \cdot \mathbf{r}_{ij})\mathbf{r}_{ij}}{(r_{ij}^2 + \epsilon^2)^{5/2}} \right], \tag{5.3}$$

where

$$\mathbf{r}_{ij} = \mathbf{x}_j - \mathbf{x}_i, \tag{5.4}$$

$$\mathbf{v}_{ij} = \mathbf{v}_j - \mathbf{v}_i. \tag{5.5}$$

Here, ϵ is the softening parameter. The first term is the usual acceleration and the second term is its time derivative. With GRAPE-4, we used the Hermite integration scheme [14, 15], for which we need the time derivative explicitly calculated. The total number of floating-point operation per one interaction is around 60, and GRAPE-4 processor chip processed three components of positions sequentially, as GRAPE-2 did. Thus, it effectively performed 20 floating-point operations per clock cycle. The total number of transistors in a GRAPE-4 chip was 400k. If we regard the 20 operations as 10 FMA operations, the number of transistors per FMA operation is 20k, three times higher than that of GRAPE-3 but still 1/6 of the actual number necessary to implement a full FP64 FMA unit. GRAPE-4 chip was designed in 1992 using 1 μm process.

GRAPE-6 [2] is the successor of GRAPE-4, designed using 0.25 μm process. Thus, we could integrate around 8M transistors, resulting in six pipelines. Each of GRAPE-6 pipelines could process one interaction per cycle. Thus, one GRAPE-6 chip effectively performed 360 floating-point operations per cycle. The transistor efficiency of GRAPE-6 is essentially the same as that of GRAPE-4.

Note that the high transistor efficiency of GRAPE processors also resulted in very high power efficiency. For example. The GRAPE-4 system comprised 1692 GRAPE-4 chips and had the nominal peak performance of 1.08 Tflops and power consumption of 12 kW. This was at 1995. In 1996, the ASCI Red became the first general-purpose machine to reach the peak performance of 1 Tflops, with 9298 Intel Pentium Pro processors. Its power consumption was 850 kW. Thus, the difference of the performance per watt was more than a factor of 50. Entire 1692 chips of GRAPE-4 were housed in four low-profile racks as shown in Fig. 5.2, while ASCI Red comprised 104 racks. This difference in the number of racks came essentially from the difference in the power consumption.

The process rule of GRAPE-4 chip was 1 μm, and the supply voltage was 5 V. The process rule for Pentium Pro was 0.5 μm, and the supply voltage was 3 V. Thus, roughly speaking, GRAPE-4 chip built with the same process technology as that for Pentium Pro would be five times more power efficient compare to the actual GRAPE-4 chip, or more than 250 times power efficient compared to Pentium Pro.

The transistor count of the processor core of Pentium Pro was 5.5M, around 14 times more than that of GRAPE-4. With this 5.5M transistors, Pentium Pro

Fig. 5.2 The GRAPE-4 system

performed one floating-point operations per cycle, while GRAPE-4 performed 20. Thus, the nominal difference in the transistor efficiency was 280, and this is very close to the difference of the power efficiency of a factor of 250.

Note that the power efficiency of recent Intel processors, when normalized for technology and supply voltage, is higher than that of Pentium Pro. The performance per watt of systems based on Pentium pro was around 2 Mflops/W. Modern Skylake-based system gives 4.5 Gflops/W. The technologies are 0.5 μm and 14 nm, different by a factor of 36 (maybe smaller due to the difference in the structure of the gate). Supply voltage of Skylake Xeon is unknown, but in the lowest case around 0.6 V. Thus, the technology and voltage difference gives at most $35 \times 5 \times 5 = 892$, while actual difference is 2250. Thus, architectural improvement is at least a factor of 2.5.

However, even if we assume the improvement of a factor of five from Pentium Pro to Skylake, a special-purpose design such as GRAPE-4 processor still gives 50 times higher power efficiency. Roughly speaking, a factor of five comes from the use of FP32 for most of operations. However, this factor of five is very difficult to achieve on general-purpose processors, even when they support FP32 SIMD operations.

If special-purpose designs is so much better than general-purpose designs, why such special-purpose designs are rare now? For molecular dynamics simulations, specialized machines such as Anton [16] and MDGRAPE-4/4A [17] have been built and the projects to develop their successors are ongoing. Of course, a huge number of specialized processors for deep learning have been developed and are being developed by a number of companies. The core of these processors are all special-purpose logic circuits for matrix-vector or matrix-matrix multiplication.

The reason why there have been not many projects to develop specialized processors, except for molecular dynamics and deep learning, is that the initial development cost of an LSI chip has become too high. In early 1990s, one could make a custom LSI chip for the initial cost of around 100K USD. This initial cost has increased exponentially in the last 30 years, and now the initial cost of an LSI chip, including the cost of IPs can be several tens of million USD. Thus, in 1990s we were able to make special-purpose processors with relatively small research grant, like a few hundred thousand USD, and actually to use them for our research. Now, we need several hundred times more money, which is certainly too large for most research projects in basic science. The cost of large ground-based telescopes are several hundred million USD, and the procurement cost of high-end supercomputers of national centers are around 200 M USDs at least in the US. Thus, projects for special-purpose computer with the total cost more than 10 M USD have become unpractical. Deep learning is an exception, with a huge and growing commercial market.

5.2   The Baseline Design: GRAPE-DR

5.2.1   Design Concept and Architecture

In this section, we discuss our GRAPE-DR processor. We started the design of GRAPE-DR in 2004. The basic concept of GRAPE-DR is an accelerator for operations such as

- interaction calculation between particles
- matrix multiplication

which can be offloaded to accelerators connected to the host processor with a relatively narrow communication path. Figure 5.3 shows the top-level structure of the GRAPE-DR processor chip. One chip contains 512 processing elements (PEs), which are organized in a two-level tree network. In the lowest level, 32 PEs (16 are shown in the figure) are connected to one "broadcast memory" (BM), and form one broadcast block (BB). The broadcast memory can broadcast the same data to all PEs under it, and at one time one of 32 PEs can send back the data to the broadcast memory. There are no connection between PEs other than the connection to the broadcast memory. BBs are connected in single-level broadcast/reduction network. The data sent from the external control processor (FPGA) can be either broadcasted to all BBs or written to one BB. The data read out from BBs can be summed (other reduction operations such as bitwise and/or, max/min can also be applied), and it is also possible to read out the data of one BB. This network structure is essentially the same as that used for GRAPE-4 or GRAPE-6.

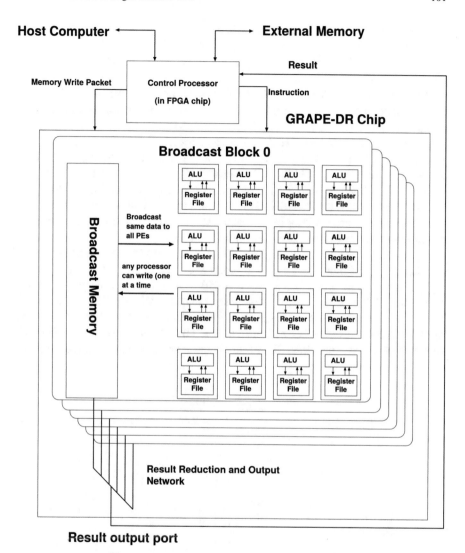

Result output port

Fig. 5.3 The structure of the GRAPE-DR processor chip

The broadcast memory is a 1k-word (double precision) dual-port memory. The floating-point word format of GRAPE-DR is nonstandard, with 72-bit double precision word and 36-bit single-precision word. A single precision word has one sign bit, 11-bit exponent and 24-bit mantissa. A double-precision word has one sign bit, 11-bit exponent and 60-bit mantissa. We chose this format since the short exponent of IEEE-754 single-precision format was inconvenient for many applications. The double-precision multiplication is done in 50-bit accuracy, by first rounding the mantissa to 50 bits. For many applications, this choice of long mantissa with small multiplier gives the accuracy better than the standard IEEE-754 double-precision format, since most of the round-off error is generated in add/subtract operations and not in multiplication operations. All data paths indicated in Fig. 5.3 have the width of 72 bits.

Note that with the design of GRAPE-DR, most of transistors are used for PEs and the fraction of transistors used for the broadcast memories and communication paths is small. One important design decision is to add a single reduction tree to BBs, but not to PEs. If we added the reduction network to PEs, its gate count is still smaller than PEs but not negligible. In addition, the width of the data path is the same everywhere. With 512 PEs, a GRAPE-DR chip performs 256 FMAs, and can read and write one double-precision words per cycle. If we count this as 16 bytes, the B/F number of GRAPE-DR is 0.0625. Our actual design had the DRAM chip with one 64-bit port, resulting in the actual B/F number of around 0.03, similar to the B/F numbers of PEZY-SC2 or Sunway SW26010.

Figure 5.4 shows the block diagram of one PE of GRAPE-DR. One PE consists of a floating-point multiplier, a floating-point adder, an integer ALU, one 32-word register file (two read and one write), one 256-word single-port memory, and one "T register". The T register is a four-word shift register. All instructions of GRAPE-DR are vector instructions with the fixed vector length of four. The T register is used to store the results of operations which are used in the successive operations so that it gives the fourth input to arithmetic units, in addition to two read ports of

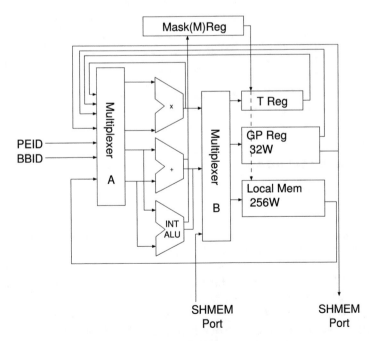

Fig. 5.4 The block diagram of one PE of GRAPE-DR processor

register file and one memory port. Also, there is a bypath from multiplier to adder, so that the result of multiplication can be fed to the adder without consuming the register port. With this feedback path and shortcut path from T-register, the results of one instruction is available to the next instruction. Thus, there is no need for loop unrolling or out-of-order execution. If the result is written to the register file or the local memory, for the next instruction the new result is not available, but available for the instruction after the next instruction.

As is shown in Fig. 5.4, the local memory is connected directly to the input and output multiplexers (A and B). Thus, we did not adopt the traditional load-store architecture. The reason why we did not adopt the load-store architecture is rather simple. First, the cycle time of on-chip single-port SRAM is the same as that of the register file. The latency is also small as long as the memory unit is physically close to the processor core. Thus, there was no need to move data to registers to perform arithmetic operations. Second, as we adopted the chip-scale SIMD architecture, it was possible to use rather long instruction word format. In addition, as we adopted the fixed-length vector instruction, the bandwidth necessary to feed the instruction is low. In the case of GRAPE-DR, the instruction was encoded into a 128-bit word, and supplied to the processor chip from a 32-bit port. With the length of 128 bits, we could specify the full address of local memory and three ports of register files, and also the operations of multiplexers and arithmetic units. In other words, a GRAPE-DR instruction was essentially the horizontal microcode, which specifies the operations of all functional blocks of a PE. For conditional execution, we added mask registers as is used in vector or recent SIMD processors, and "indirect addressing" was also possible using the T register.

Note that this long instruction format and the use of vector instruction eliminated the need for "advanced" features such as superscalar execution, out-of-order execution, register renaming, and branch prediction.

One might think the choice to use the fixed-length vector instruction would have resulted in too many hardware-level parallelism. In practice, this is not the case. A single GRAPE-DR processor already has 512 processors anyway. Most of problems for which we want to use GRAPE-DR have much larger level of parallelism. Also, when we have a double loop as in the case of particle-particle interaction or triple loop as in the case of matrix multiplication, the reduction network made it possible to parallelize the loops of different levels with very low overhead.

For example, consider the loop structure like Listing 5.1. Here, we assume p[i] represents a structure (or class) for particle i, p[i].a is the acceleration of particle i, and f(p1, p2) is a function which takes two arguments and returns the acceleration on p1 from p2. We can parallelize this loop over both indices i and j, but parallelization over j requires the reduction of partial results. After the partial results are calculated on different processors, we need to take reductions through interprocessor communications. On machines with hierarchical cache, this reduction can take very long time since the latency of communication through cache memory is rather large and thus the throughput become small. However, with GRAPE-DR, this reduction is done with the latency of a few tens of clock cycles and the bandwidth the same as that for reading the data in one BB. Thus, we can use the two-level parallelism without worrying about the latency of the reduction. As a result, the degree of parallelism we need at one level, in this case nj, is much smaller than the total number of PEs, even though we use the fixed-length vector instructions.

The matrix-matrix multiplication has the triple-loop structure, and we can apply a similar technique so that the calculation of one element is distributed over multiple PEs in different BBs, and the reduction network is used to obtain the final result.

Listing 5.1 Example of double loop

```
for (j=0; j< nj; j++){
  for (i=0; i< ni; i++){
    p[i].a += f(p[i], p[j]);
  }
}
```

Concerning the DRAM access, GRAPE-DR did not provide any way for individual PEs to access DRAM. Only the block data transfer to/from BMs was supported. This design made the hardware extremely simple and efficient. On the other hand, this choice clearly made it difficult to port existing programs. For the initial design targets of GRAPE-DR, an accelerator for the calculation of particle-particle interactions and matrix multiplication, this was not really a limitation since even though they consume a large fraction of the computing time, almost all lines of the application code do other things. In the case of matrix-matrix multiplication, GRAPE-DR is used to accelerate the DGEMM function of the BLAS library. In the case of particle-particle simulation, the function to use GRAPE-DR replaces the call to previous generations of GRAPE hardware.

An obvious, but not well appreciated, advantage of the chip-scale SIMD architecture is that the there is no need for the synchronization operation, since all PEs are always synchronized. The barrier synchronization is a rather expensive operation on shared-memory multiprocessors. For example, the overhead of a very highly optimized implementation of the barrier synchronization on the Intel Xeon Phi was $6\,\mu s$ [18]. This is of the order of 10^4 clock cycles, Thus, in order to make the overhead of the barrier synchronization small enough, processor cores need to execute at least 10^5, and preferably 10^6, instructions between barriers. With such a large overhead, it is unpractical to apply the parallelization strategy we used for GRAPE-DR, and thus the maximum performance we can achieve for one function (for example, one matrix-matrix multiplication) by parallelization is generally much higher for SIMD parallel processors than for MIMD parallel processors.

Of course, it is possible to implement a low-latency core-to-core communication path, as in the cases of Cray parallel vector processors or Sunway SW26010, or to add hardware support for the barrier synchronization as in the case of Fujitsu A64fx. However, it is unpractical to add such hardware support to manycore processors with cache. The hardware barrier of A64fx is available to processors in the same CMG (which share the same L2 cache). Neither Cray parallel vector processors nor SW26010 have data caches. PEZY-SC processors are unique and they support the

Fig. 5.5 The GRAPE-DR processor card with four GRAPE-DR processor chips

synchronization operation at each level of the cache. However, this is again a rather expensive operation, associated with the cache flush (Fig. 5.7).

Figure 5.5 shows the GRAPE-DR processor board with four GRAPE-DR chip. Each GRAPE-DR chips (four larger chips) are connected to FPGA chips (four smaller chips), which have the PCIe interface and DRAM interface. Four FPGA chips are connected in a ring network, and also connected to a PLX 8632 PCIe switch, which convert four four-lane PCIe gen2 links to a single 16-lane link. The card size is nonstandard, but the interface itself is standard PCIe.

Figure 5.6 shows the entire GRAPE-DR system with 128 host computers each with two GRAPE-DR cards.

5.2.2 The Efficiency

The gate count of one PE of GRAPE-DR is 110k. Thus the nominal transistor count is 440k. It performed one double-precision FMA operation in every two clock cycles. With the nominal transistor count of 12k for one FMA, the transistor efficiency of GRAPE-DR is 13.6%.

Figure 5.7 shows the layout of one PE. The actual size is 0.7 mm by 0.7 mm. The area with the orange color is the floating-point multiplier. We can see that the

Fig. 5.6 The GRAPE-DR system

efficiency of 13.6% is not far off from the actual area. A large area is occupied by the register file. This is because we could not use a memory macro for the register file and it was implemented using random gates. The area occupied by the local memory is quite small. This is simply because its size is actually very small. Intel i860XP had 12KB or on-chip memory, while one PE of GRAPE-DR only 2KB (or actually 2.25KB). However, the total size of local memories on one processor chip is 1 MB, which is large enough to reduce the amount of memory access for matrix multiplication.

Concerning the power efficiency, GRAPE-DR system achieved 1.45 Gflops/W in HPL, and ranked No. 2 in the November 2010 Green500 list. The No. 1 machine was prototype BlueGene/Q, with 1.68 Gflops/W. GRAPE-DR chip was fabricated using 90 nm technology, while BlueGene/Q 45 nm. BlueGene/Q remained at the top of the Green500 list until November 2012, when Intel Xeon Phi 5110P, fabricated with 22 nm technology, took the place. Thus, we can conclude the power efficiency of the GRAPE-DR processor chip was exceptionally high, with efficiency competitive to those of processors fabricated with semiconductor technologies two or three generations later. We believe it is not unfair to say that the power efficiency of the design of the GRAPE-DR processor was significantly higher than that of processors of the same time. This is not surprising since the transistor efficiency of GRAPE-DR is quite high. We have reviewed most of high-performance processors of the last half century, and only CM-2 and GRAPE-DR achieved the transistor efficiency higher than 10%.

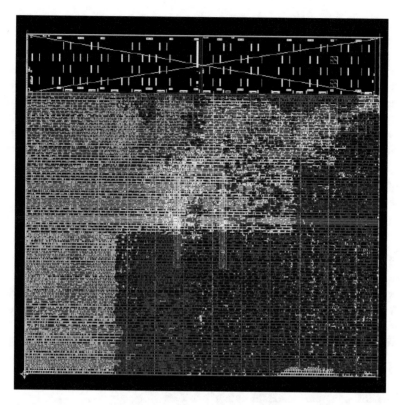

Fig. 5.7 The design of one PE of GRAPE-DR. Orange, green, blue and red areas are used for floating-point multiplier, floating-point adder, integer ALU, and the register file. The black rectangle at the top is the memory macro for the local memory (72 bit 256 words)

Actually, we have designed GRAPE-DR with the design of CM-2, in particular after its interpretation was changed to 32-bit processors with FPU, in mind. Therefore it is quite natural that there are many similarities.

We here summarize the efficiencies for matrix-matrix multiplication and particle-particle interaction. For the matrix-matrix multiplication, the measured performance was 90% of the theoretical peak [4]. Roughly half of the loss came from the startup time of the calculation on GRAPE-DR, and another half from the dead time for the replacement of one of the two input matrices. The communication for the other matrix was fully overlapped with the calculation. The startup time of the calculation kernel of GRAPE-DR was around 10 μs. It was necessary to write several registers in the control processor from the host computer using PIO (program I/O) operation. Sending one word through PIO takes the time of the order of 1 μs. We could have shorten this overhead by several methods. One is to minimize the number of PIO writes we need to start the computing kernel. By clever encoding and also by having a table of kernels and DMA parameters on the control processors, it is not difficult to start the kernel with single PIO write. Another possibility is just to make the one call to kernel longer, by combining multiple calls. Since the efficiency of 90% is practically sufficient, we had not tried too hard to further improve the efficiency. This startup overhead is comparable to that of modern Cuda kernels.

For the particle-particle interaction, the achieved efficiency was limited by the number of operations we need to calculate the inverse square root, which is necessary for most of interaction calculations. GRAPE-DR lacked the hardwired logic to obtain the initial guess for the inverse square root. Almost all modern processors have hardware support for this initial guess, with either 8 bit or 12–13 bit accuracy. From these initial guess, single step of Newton-Raphson iteration or its third-order version is sufficient to obtain the single-precision value, which is sufficient for many applications. With GRAPE-DR, we had to use a sequence of integer operations to obtain a low-order estimate.

5.2.3 Software

As we stated already, we have designed GRAPE-DR and its control processor with only two types of application in mind: the calculation of particle-particle interactions and matrix-matrix multiplication.

This design choice made the necessary software rather simple and limited. For the calculation of particle-particle interaction, GRAPE-DR would "emulate" previous GRAPE processors. Thus, the basic operation would be the following.

1. The host computer sends the data of particles
2. GRAPE-DR calculates the interactions between particles and sends them back to the host computer.

The actual implementation is more complicated since we need to take into account things like the use of individual timestep scheme as in GRAPE-4/6 [19], use of multiple PEs, and also the use of the tree algorithm [20], but the program code on PE is quite simple. Thus, the use of the assembly language was sufficient to develop kernels.

The same was true for matrix-matrix multiplication. In this case, the optimized kernel was generated automatically by a simple script.

Writing the kernel in the assembly language was relatively simple on GRAPE-DR, because of the following two features. First, the instruction latency was hidden by the vector instruction set. Therefore, there was no need for techniques such as loop unrolling or software pipelining, since the result of one instruction was always available to the next instruction. Second, the entire local memory could be specified as an operand for any operation. Therefore, in most cases we do not need any load/store operation, and thus the number of instructions necessary to express a kernel is small.

Of course, the initial learning curve for a new assembly language is high, and eventually two compilers were developed. The first one, LSUMP[21], translated the description of interaction calculation written in a simple DSL (Domain-specific language) to GRAPE-DR assembly code. It also generated the API for the host program to transfer data and start the GRAPE-DR kernel, so that application programmers could use these generate APIs.

Listing 5.2 shows an example of the kernel written in LSUMP. Here, the three keywords, VARI, VARJ and VARF, specify the data for particles which receive the force, particles that exert the force, and the calculated force itself. In this example everything is in double precision.

Listing 5.2 Example of particle-particle interaction written in LSUMP

```
/VARI xi, yi, zi, e2;
/VARJ xj, yj, zj, mj;
/VARF fx, fy, fz;
dx = xi - xj;
dy = yi - yj;
dz = zi - zj;
r2 = dx*dx + dy*dy + dz*dz + e2;
r1i = powm12(r2);
r3i = r1i*r1i*r1i;
ff = mj*r3i;
fx += dx*ff;
fy += dy*ff;
fz += dz*ff;
```

The Goose compiler [22] was built on top of LSUMP. Listing 5.3 shows an example of particle-particle interaction written in Goose. The Goose compiler takes usual C code with #pragma goose as input, and recognizes the double-loop structure and converts it to LSUMP kernel code and calls to the generated API functions.

Listing 5.3 Example of particle-particle interaction written in Goose

```
#pragma goose parallel for loopcounter(i, j) precision("double")
    for (i = 0; i < n; i++) {
        for (j = 0; j < n; j++) {
            for (k = 0; k < 3; k++) {
                dx[k] = x[j][k] - x[i][k];
            }
            r2 = dx[0] * dx[0] + dx[1] * dx[1] +
                dx[2] * dx[2] + eps2;
            rinv = rsqrt(r2);
            mrinv = m[j] * rinv;
            mr3inv = mrinv * rinv * rinv;
            for (k = 0; k < 3; k++) {
                a[i][k] += mr3inv * dx[k];
            }
            pot[i] -= mrinv;
        }
    }
```

LSUMP has been further extended to generate Cuda kernels and also HDL code for FPGA. This approach "solved" the problem of so-called performance portability at least for applications for which LSUMP can be used. Here, the problem of the performance portability is that a program optimized for one architecture, even when written fully in a compiler language, is not optimal for another architecture.

Moreover, in many cases the application programmers are forced to use either assembly code or so-called "intrinsics" to take advantage of SIMD units of modern processors. The intrinsics are functions recognized by compilers and translated to machine instructions almost directly. It is supported by major compilers (GCC, CLANG, and the Intel compiler). Each SIMD architecture has its set of intrinsics. In the case of Intel CPUs, SSE, AVX, AVX2, and AVX512 all have different set of intrinsics and thus porting a kernel written for SSE to AVX implies rewriting the entire code. The usual code written in high-level language is of course portable, but compilers are not clever enough to make the best use of each instruction set. Also, the way the parallelization over multiple cores and cache blocking are used is different on different processors, and an application programmer need to be aware of such differences.

This lack of the performance portability has been a rather serious problem on modern multicore processors with SIMD execution units and hierarchical caches. If the application programmer of one application has to take care of multiple architectures, he/she need to be familiar with optimization techniques for multiple architectures. This is becoming impractical even for just Intel x86, since there are already too many SIMD instruction set.

With LSUMP, only the developer of LSUMP need to know about optimization techniques of different architectures. Moreover, since we can define a clear interface between the parser and the code generator, it is relatively easy to add the support for a new architecture.

One very important implication of this approach is that the parallelization strategy is hidden in the code generation algorithm of LSUMP and the application programmer need not know about the details of the architecture of the processor he/she wants to use. Of course, this very good feature is limited to the kernel routines for heavy calculations such as particle-particle interaction calculation and matrix multiplications, but these kernels dominate the total calculation time and thus it is in many cases sufficient if very highly optimized kernels are available just for these functions.

We can see that LSUMP is, at as far as the intention of the designer is concerned, really a DSL targeted only to the calculation of particle-particle interaction. However, it turned out that it can be used for other class of applications. For example, many trivially parallel simulations or numerical integrations can be done, and thus Goose/LSUMP has been applied to problems other than particle-based simulations [23, 24].

5.3   Functions Necessary to Widen Application Area

In the previous section. we saw that, as far as particle-based simulations and matrix-matrix multiplications are concerned, the necessary software for GRAPE-DR is rather simple, since the functions it has to perform are limited. In other words, with the approach in the previous section,we apply GRAPE-DR only to the limited "hot spots" of a limited range of applications. Of course, this is the simple and effective way to use accelerator hardware of any type, either it is GRAPE, GPGPU, or FPGA. We can call this approach the offloading model, since we let the accelerator hardware perform only the hot spots and let the host CPU perform the rest of the calculation.

Naturally we should ask two questions.

(a) Is it sufficient to apply accelerators only to hot spots?
(b) Can accelerators be applied to applications of categories other than particles and dense matrices?

These two questions are not independent, since calculations with particles and dense matrices have clear hot spots. On the other hand, there are overhead associated with the offloading model. One is the communication overhead and the other is the fact that the host CPU is slower than the accelerator (if not, there is no reason to use accelerators).

5.3.1 Particles

For particle-based simulations, we have made a detailed analysis of the distribution of the calculation time for the offloading model, not for GRAPE-DR but for a modern GPGPU, NVIDIA TITAN V, connected to Intel Xeon E5-2670 v3 [25]. Our analysis is limited to the Barnes-Hut tree algorithm. However, if schemes like FMM is used, the general characteristics of the calculation cost would be largely similar. Therefore here we summarize some of our findings.

The theoretical peak performance of NVIDIA TITAN V for single-precision operations is 13.8 Tflops, while that of Intel Xeon E5-2670 v3 is 883 Gflops. Thus, ideally the speedup by a factor of around 15 should be achieved. What we found is that the best speedup we achieved is around a factor of 10, and that can only be achieved with a new scheme which reduces the amount of the work of the host CPU.

In the traditional implementation of the Barnes-Hut tree algorithm, the tree is constructed from scratch at each timestep, and the force calculation is done by traversing this newly built tree. Both the tree construction and the tree traversal are performed by the host CPU, and these operations limit the speedup factor possible with the simple offloading to around a factor of two, even though the accelerator is faster by a factor of 15.

We have implemented what we call the reusing scheme, which is similar to the neighbor list (or bookkeeping) scheme used in molecular dynamics. The basic idea of this scheme is to "reuse" the results of the tree construction and the tree traversal for multiple timesteps. In molecular dynamics, this scheme works very well since the timescale at which the molecules move is long compared to the timestep determined by the stability criterion. In astrophysics, in some cases it works well. In some other cases, particles move the distance of the order of, or even larger than, the typical interparticle distance. In such cases the reusing scheme does not work well.

On the other hand, even though the communication between the host and accelerator is through a relatively narrow PCI Express link, it was not a serious bottleneck. In addition, as far as the reusing scheme can be used, improvement of the speed of the accelerator gives the further speedup of the entire calculation, for example, a accelerator four times faster would give the speedup of a factor of 3.5.

Thus, for many real applications, the reusing scheme works fine and the offloading model can be used even when the difference in the speed is as large as a factor of 40. On the other hand, there are applications for which the reusing scheme cannot be used. One example is the pure gravitational N-body problem, where particles (which represent stars or dark matter particles) interact with other particles only through gravity. Even though one particle feel the forces from neighbor particles, in one timestep particles usually move the distance of the order of the interparticle distance. We allow this behavior either by the use of potential softening, which "soften" the gravitational force for the distance of the order of the interparticle distance, or through the use of hybrid integration scheme [26], in which the gravitational force between two particles is split into near and far terms, and only the far term is integrated using the global timestep. For such a problem, we need to accelerate both the tree construction and the tree traversal.

The most expensive operation in the tree construction procedure is sorting. Sorting on large-scale SIMD processors have been studied well on CM-2 [27] and DAP [28]. On CM-2 the sample sort turned out to be the fastest, though the bitonic sort [29] can be implemented more easily and the radix sort can also be used.

From the theoretical point of view, it is not surprising that the sample sort is the fastest on most of distributed-memory parallel computers. In any parallel sorting algorithm, the data in one processor should be moved to many other processors. The basic idea of the sample sort is to determine which data would go to which processor using sampling and then let all processors send data directly to their final destinations. Thus, there is essentially no redundant data move, and the communication time is the smallest for the sample sort.

The minimum requirement of the sample sort is that there must be some mechanism for each PE to send data to the destination PE in a data-dependent way. CM-2 had the quite flexible hypercube network, which allowed such data-dependent communications. We need to investigate what would be the simplest network which allows the implementation of the sample sort.

The advantage of the bitonic sort is that its communication pattern is fixed. Thus, it is much easier to design an on-chip network suitable for the bitonic sort. The performance of these sorting algorithms are determined essentially by the off-chip memory bandwidth if the particles do not fit into the on-chip memory, and the bisection bandwidth of the on-chip network if they fit into the on-chip memory. Off-chip sample sort can be implemented with the memory access of two reads and two writes.

The tree traversal is not easy to implement on large-scale SIMD machine. On CM-2, we have implemented the Barnes-Hut algorithm, and achieved a reasonable performance [30]. We relied on the powerful and flexible hypercube network, and converted the tree structure to a fat tree, so that the congestion of access to high-level tree nodes could be avoided.

In the traditional tree algorithm, each particle (or each group or particles), traverse the tree. The traversal itself can be done in parallel, and thus there are sufficient degree of parallelism. However, each traversal involves pointer chasing, and thus quite inefficient on modern machines with large memory access latency.

Here, we propose a different approach for the tree traversal. In this approach, we traverse the tree for many particles or groups. In the usual parallel implementation, different particles traverse the tree independently. In our new approach, all particles follow the same path, but calculate the interaction only when necessary. Conceptually, the stack-less iterative tree traversal [31] is given in Listing 5.4.

Listing 5.4   Pseudocode for stack-less iterative tree walk for one particle

```
node = root
while node != NULL)
   if node and particle are well separated
      calculate the force from the node
      node = next[node]
   else
      node = first_child[node]
   end
end
```

In the stack-less iterative tree traversal, instead of the usual recursion or the emulation of the recursion with the stack, we add two pointers to each tree node, next and first_child. The next pointer points to the node for which the recursive algorithm would reach after the force from that node is evaluated. The first_child pointer points to the node for which the recursive algorithm would reach after we decide to go down the tree.

Listing 5.5 shows our new approach. Instead of the pointer chasing, we just walk through the tree in the depth-first order. The next_in_tree pointer thus point to the location of the next node when all nodes are listed in the order of depth-first walk. If the nodes are reordered in the depth-first ordering, no pointer access is involved here.

The basic idea of our new approach is that at each node, we calculate the interaction to particles for which the force calculation is necessary. The judgment is done through the active flag and next pointer. Once one interaction calculation is done, that particle is made inactive unless the tree walk reaches next node.

Listing 5.5   Pseudocode of stack-less iterative tree walk for multiple particles

```
node = root
for each particle
   active[particle] =true
end
while (node != NULL){
   for each inactive particle
      if next[particle] == node
```

```
            active[particle]=true
         end
      end
      for each active particle
         if  node and particle are well separated
            calculate the force from the node
            active[particle]=false
            next[particle] = next[node]  (
         end
      end
      node = next_in_tree[node]
   end
```

A naive implementation of this algorithm involves $O(N^2)$ calculation, since the test for the current node is done for all inactive particles each time. On usual general-purpose computers, this can be eliminated by maintaining the list of particles to be activated for each node. Since we traverse the tree in the depth-first order, this list can be implemented as a stack.

On chip-scale SIMD processors, this is usually not a serious problem since the number of particles handled by one chip is much smaller than the total number of particles in the system. We first create the tree good enough to calculate the force on all particles on the processor chip, and then apply this algorithm. In this case, the calculation cost of the judgment is $O(n^2)$, where n is the number of particles handled by one chip. In other words, the total cost is $O(Nn)$, not $O(N^2)$, with a small coefficient. Thus, usually we can expect that this part does not dominate the total cost. The only "communication" function we need to implement this algorithm is the broadcasting of the tree node data to all PEs. The main memory is accessed only once per tree node.

Thus, the two key operations, sorting and tree traversal, can both be implemented on chip-scale SIMD processors with reasonable efficiencies. The amount of memory access per particle per timestep is $O(10)$, while the calculation cost of the interaction is around $O(10^5)$. This means we could use a processor with the B/F number of order of 0.001, nearly two orders of magnitude smaller than the actual B/F numbers of most of modern microprocessors.

5.3.2   Dense Matrices

As of early 2020s, the most widely used application of the operations of dense matrices is the deep learning, and in particular convolutional neural network (CNN).

Very roughly, in the case of image recognition, the idea of CNN is the following. We start from a two-dimensional neuron array corresponding to the input image, and first move to three-dimensional array and then go back to the original two dimensional structure. It is called convolutional because the neural network works as a convolutional filter on the output of the previous layer. The same "filter" coefficients are applied to each "pixel" (in many cases 3×3 images) to obtain the input value for the next layer. Each "pixel" has the "depth" direction, and for this direction full matrix-vector multiplication is applied. The matrix for the coefficients is the same for all input pixels, and thus we can express the application of coefficients as the matrix-matrix multiplication.

The maximum depth of the networks used now is around 2048. Therefore, if we store the output of internal layers of CNN to the external memory, we can only do around 2000 operations per one read and one write, or 1000 operations per memory access. If we do everything in half precision (FP16), we need the minimum B/F number of 0.002. If we design the processor core so that the peak performance of FP16 operation is 16 times higher than that of FP64 operation, this B/F number corresponds to 0.032 for FP64 operations. This number is only for layers with the largest depth, and several layers have smaller depths. Thus, very roughly, CNNs at present require the B/F number of around 0.1.

Note that this memory access is required for the learning through the backward error propagation. In order to calculate the error in the intermediate layers, the value calculated in the inference phase must be stored. Thus, if we have layers $0, 1, \ldots n - 1$, we need to read inputs of all layers for the backward error propagation.

If we store the data for only layers $0, 2, 4, \ldots$, we can reduce the memory access by a factor of two, but we have to recalculate the values for layers $1, 3, \ldots$, and thus the cost of the forward calculation increases by 50%. This increase is usually acceptable, since the cost of the backward calculation is two or three times higher than that of the forward calculation anyway. If we make this interval of two larger, we can further reduce the memory access by a factor proportional to the interval s, but the calculation cost increase roughly as s^2.

If we can store the data for $O(\log s)$ layers in the on-chip memory, we can reduce the cost of re-calculation to $O(\log s)$, by applying the recursion. If $s = 4$, we first calculate the value at layer 2, keep it, and then calculate layer 3, and finally layer 1. The total calculation cost is 4. For $s = 8$, we first go to layer 4, and apply the process for $s = 4$, and then repeat the same process for layers 1 to 3. Thus, the calculation cost C_{k+1} for $s = 2^{k+1}$ is given by

$$C_{k+1} = 2C_k + 2^k. \tag{5.6}$$

To solve this recurrence relation, we introduce a new series by

$$x_k = C_k/2^k. \tag{5.7}$$

We have

$$x_{k+1} = x_k + 1/2. \tag{5.8}$$

Thus we can see that x_k is $O(k)$ and C_k is $O(s \log s)$, and that the cost of recalculation per layer is $O(\log s)$.

The recalculation cost of $O(\log s)$ is usually acceptable, but whether or not the sufficient amount of the on-chip memory is available is a different question.

Another issue is that the total size of the coefficients (so-called "weights" of the network) is large. The total number of parameters for ResNet-50 is 2.5×10^7. Thus, if expressed in the single precision format, the data size is 104 MB. In the back propagation phase, these weights must be updated to achieve learning. If we use multiple processors for learning, the reduction of the updates over all processors should be performed and then the updated weights must be shared. In multi-GPU calculations, this part, which is usually implemented with MPI_ALLREDUCE call, forms the bottleneck. Usual approach to solve this problem is to increase the number of images (the size of the minibatch.) With this approach, we can increase the calculation cost per minibatch, and thus reduce the necessary bandwidth for the MPI_ALLREDUCE operation.

This increase of the size of the minibatch makes it difficult to use the recalculation strategy we just described, since recalculation requires that the processor can keep $O(\log s)$ layers of the part of the minibatch to be processed on it. If the minibatch size is very large, it is not possible to apply this strategy.

Let us evaluate the relation between the performance of the processor, necessary bandwidth for communication, necessary bandwidth for the memory access, and the required amount of the memory.

For simplicity, we assume the depth of the network is $d = 1000$, and we apply 1×1 filter. The calculation time is given by

$$T_{\text{calc}} = 2nd^2\tau_{\text{calc}}, \tag{5.9}$$

where n is the total number of pixels in one minibatch processed on a processor and τ_{calc} is the time to perform one floating point operation. The communication time is given by

$$T_{\text{comm}} = d^2\tau_{\text{comm}}, \tag{5.10}$$

where τ_{comm} is the time to communicate one word. We assume an ideal pipelined communication network in which the reduction operation can be processed at the speed of the local network port. The amount of the memory we need to keep pixel data is given by

$$N_{\text{p}} = nd \log s, \tag{5.11}$$

and the time to read/write the off-chip memory is given by

$$T_{\text{mem}} = \frac{2nd\tau_{\text{mem}}}{s}. \tag{5.12}$$

Thus, if we require that T_{comm} and T_{mem} are smaller than T_{calc}, we have

$$\frac{\tau_{\text{comm}}}{\tau_{\text{calc}}} < 2n, \tag{5.13}$$

and

$$\frac{\tau_{mem}}{\tau_{calc}} < ds. \tag{5.14}$$

For example, consider a processor with the peak speed of 1PF, the communication speed of 100 GB/s, and the memory access speed of 100 GB/s. We have $\tau_{calc} = 10^{-15}$, $\tau_{comm} = 2 \times 10^{-11}$, $\tau_{mem} = 2 \times 10^{-11}$, and $d = 1000$. Thus,

$$n > 10^4, \tag{5.15}$$

and

$$s > 20, \tag{5.16}$$

The total amount of on-chip memory necessary is $N_p = nd \log s = 10^7 \log s$. This is less than 100 MB.

To achieve the performance of 1PF, assuming the clock speed of 1 GHz, we need 5×10^5 FP units. Thus, we need 1600 bits of memory, around 10k transistors per FP unit. The required accuracy is small, like 8–10 bit mantissa. thus, the number of transistors necessary is much smaller than our standard 120k for double-precision operation. If we assume 6k transistors, the numbers of transistors for memory and that for arithmetic units roughly balance. In practice, somewhat larger memory size would be acceptable, since the size of the SRAM is significantly smaller than that of multiplier logic if the number of the transistor is the same.

From inequality 5.13, we can see that the necessary amount of memory is determined by the ratio between the communication bandwidth and the calculation speed, and is actually larger for larger network depth (larger d). This result might be a bit counter-intuitive, since larger d implies larger calculation cost per pixel. However, what is communicated here is the weights and their total data size is proportional to d^2. Thus, even though the calculation cost increases for larger d, the communication cost increases even faster, and the necessary amount of memory increases.

If we increase the effective communication bandwidth, we can reduce the necessary amount of the on-chip memory. Since the learning process is stochastic, we should be able to apply various lossy data compression techniques. There are other operations which require global communications, such as the batch normalization. However, the necessary communication bandwidth is small (latency can be dominant).

From inequality 5.13, we can see that by making s large, we can reduce the necessary memory bandwidth, without too much impact on the performance or the necessary size of the on-chip memory. Our estimate here is probably a bit optimistic, since we ignore the effect of layers with small d near the initial and final layers. The contribution of these layers depends on the details of the network structure. Therefore, it is desirable to make the bandwidth to the external memory reasonably high. For example, if there is a single layer with $d = 16$ and 3×3 filter, the required B/F number for FP16 operation is around 0.005, corresponding to 0.08 for FP64 operation. If we require 10% efficiency for these layers, the necessary B/F is 0.008. For FP16 operation, the necessary B/F number is around 0.0005. For the peak performance of 1PF, this is 500 GB/s.

To summarize, with current CNN, the design requirement for processors are

- There are the tradeoff between the communication speed and the size of the on-chip memory. Very roughly, for 1PF processor, 100 GB/s network and 100 MB memory. If the network is faster by a factor of two, we can reduce the size of the memory by the same factor of two.
- A reasonable memory bandwidth is preferred. (B/F = 0.01 for FP 64 operation)

5.3.3 Other Applications

In the previous section, we discussed the possibility to use chip-scale SIMD processors to run particle-based and dense-matrix applications. We have seen that the additional functions required are not very complex and can be added without loosing the transistor efficiency and thus power efficiency too much. In this section, we discuss what is necessary for applications of other categories. We do not discuss the random graphs since their requirements are rather similar to those of unstructured mesh calculations.

5.3.3.1 Structured Mesh

Calculations using structured mesh had been the primary target of large-scale SIMD processors like Illiac IV, Goodyear MPP and ICL DAP. Thus, we can safely conclude that to use chip-scale SIMD processors for structured-mesh calculations is straightforward. The design of GRAPE-DR lacks the two-dimensional mesh connection which most of large-scale SIMD processors had. Thus, it is necessary to design the communication network so that it has sufficient bandwidth for nearest neighbor communications. In addition, if the external memory bandwidth is very small (BF ≪ 0.01), we need to consider the possibility to implement the temporal blocking scheme [32–34], and the memory access mechanism must be flexible enough to support it.

5.3.3.2 Unstructured Mesh

As we have already discussed in Sect. 3.4, it is probably unpractical to consider the possibility of use external memory as the main storage for iterative solvers used with unstructured mesh. Even on machines with very high external memory bandwidth like A64fx, the efficiency of iterative solvers is very low, of the order of a few percents. With much lower relative memory bandwidth, it is impossible to achieve high efficiency. On the other hand, if all necessary data are in the on-chip memory, very high efficiency is possible, since the B/F number of the local memory of PEs is very high.

Here, one practical problem is how we distribute the mesh data over PEs and how let them communicate data. With usual domain decomposition, domains are not necessarily mapped to grid, and thus PEs need to communicate through general-purpose routing network such as the hypercube network of CM-2. On the other hand, if we can construct the domain decomposition which can be mapped to the network topology of the processor hardware, we do not need the routing network. The hardware cost of the routing network would be relatively small, since the necessary bandwidth is not very high. Even so, the amount of human resources necessary to design and test the router can be very high, in particular because the design of the rest of the chip is rather simple. An important advantage of chip-scale SIMD processors is that the design is very simple. The routing network adds the asynchronous execution and makes the design much more complex.

Another potential problem is that we do need fairly fast interconnect between processor chips, as we have discussed in Sect. 3.4. The necessary bandwidth is rather similar to the bandwidth necessary for the deep learning applications, and thus might not be unpractical.

5.3.3.3 Summary

We have seen that chip-scale SIMD processors can be applied to most of important applications. Unstructured mesh calculations seem to be most difficult, since they do need rather flexible routing network if implemented naively. For other applications, much simpler communication patterns such as nearest neighbors in regular grids and reduction/broadcast over the tree network seem to be sufficient.

The support for the reduction/broadcast over the tree network, combined with the SIMD execution model, makes fine-grain parallelism much easier to implement compared to MIMD shared-memory multiprocessors on which the interprocessor communication is through coherent caches. The synchronization of cores on a MIMD multiprocessor can take multiple microseconds, while the reduction through hardwired reduction network on a SIMD processor can be done in a few tens of machine cycles, of the order of a few tens of nanoseconds. Thus, the overhead associated with distributing calculation over multiple processors on a SIMD processor is around 100 times smaller than that for a MIMD processor. This characteristic is particularly useful for particles and dense matrices, where very large degree of parallelism is available if the cost of the reduction over a large number of cores is small.

5.4   An Extreme for Deep Learning: MN-Core/GRAPE-PFN

In this section, we briefly discuss the MN-Core processor, a chip-scale SIMD processor the author jointly developed with Preferred Networks. It is also called as GRAPE-PFN, showing the two origins of the processor.

The details of the chip will be given elsewhere. Here, we summarize the performance numbers and basic architecture. Tables 5.1 and 5.2 give the overview of MN-Core and comparison with GRAPE-DR.

Compared to GRAPE-DR, the FP64 performance of MN-Core is increased by a factor of 128. For a single die, the relative improvement is a factor of 32. This is reasonable, albeit a bit modest, considering the advance of the semiconductor technology from 90 nm to a smaller feature size. The total power consumption of a package with four dies is 500 W. Here, we assume that the power consumption of one die is around 125 W. The FP64 performance per watt is thus around 66 GF/W. This looks like an extremely high number. The actual measured performance-per-watt number for HPL is around 30 GF/W, which is reasonable if we take into account the factors such as the relatively low measured application efficiency, other losses in the power supply, and the power consumption of the host computer. The performance-per-watt number of GRAPE-DR is around 4 GF/W. Thus, MN-Core achieved 15 times better power efficiency.

The dynamic power consumption of CMOS gates is proportional to the size of the design rule, if the power supply voltage is the same and the structure of the gate is the same. The move from planar "bulk" CMOS gate to the three-dimensional FinFET structure *increased* the power consumption, since the gate capacitance is increased. In addition, the size of the transistor used in, for example, TSMC's 16FF+ process is not 16/90 of TSMC's 90 nm process, because the transistor size of 16FF+ is the same as that of TSMC's bulk 20 nm process. Thus, the reduction in the gate capacitance is less than a factor of 4.5. With N7 process, this factor is probably around 6 or 7. On the other hand, this move made the operation with lower supply voltage possible, resulting in much lower power consumption. Thus, a factor of 20 improvement from GRAPE-DR is not impossible, but not easy. Clearly, the change in the PE architecture contributed to the improved performance.

Table 5.1 The overview of MN-Core

FP16 peak performance	524.3 TF
FP32 peak performance	131.1 TF
FP64 peak performance	32.8 TF
Number of dies in a package	4

Table 5.2 MN-Core and GRAPE-DR

	GRAPE-DR	MN-Core
Design rule	90 nm	–
FP64 peak performance	256 GF	8.192 TF (per die)
Power consumption	65 W	~125 W (per die)
FP64 watt-performance	3.9 GF/W	~66 GF/W

The main difference of PE architectures between GRAPE-DR and MN-Core is that the latter is specialized to matrix-vector multiplication. The size of matrix is not given in public material yet, but the fact that the FP32 peak performance is four times that of FP64, and FP16 is four times that of FP32 means the matrix sizes for FP32 and FP16 are two and four times larger than that for FP64.

Another difference is that we added one more level to the on-chip network. GRAPE-DR had three-level tree network. The bottom layer is PEs, the first level is BB (broadcast blocks), and the top level is the chip itself with broadcast/reduction to BBs. In MN-Core, there are level-1 BBs and level-2 BBs. The operations and bandwidth of these BBs have been designed carefully to meet the requirement of deep-learning applications.

All in all, MN-Core is a natural extension of GRAPE-DR for deep learning designed with more advanced technology. The design concept is largely similar, and the primary difference is the support for the matrix-vector multiplication operation.

5.5 A "General-Purpose" Design

In Sect. 5.3, we have discussed what functionalities would be necessary if we want to use a chip-scale SIMD processor for a wide range of applications. They are the followings.

- On-chip network which supports sorting (bitonic sort is acceptable).
- off-chip DRAM access mechanism flexible enough to support the temporal blocking for structured-mesh calculations.
- chip-to-chip communication network fast enough to support both deep learning and unstructured-mesh calculations.
- Support for FP64, FP32 and FP16 or other mixed-precision operations, such as matrix-vector multiplication on FP16 with results in FP32.

In this section, we present a rough estimate of the power and area consumption of circuits to realize these functionalities.

5.5.1 On-Chip Network for Sorting

Sorting appears in many applications. One example is particle-based simulations, where sorting is used to construct the octree structure. If the size of the dataset is larger than that of the on-chip memory, the sample sort offers near-optimal performance, if its performance is limited by the off-chip memory access bandwidth and not by some other bottleneck. Thus, the question is how we can implement off-chip sample sort with a chip-scale SIMD architecture, without making the cost of the on-chip network too high.

The basic idea of the sample sort is the following. Consider the case we use p PEs to sort the data of size N. We can first divide the data to p subset, $s_1, \ldots s_p$, such that $x < y$, if $x \in s_i$, $y \in s_j$, and $i < j$. Then all PEs sort its own subset. In order to make the initial division of data, we need to know the boundary values of b_i for s_i and s_{i+1}. We estimate these boundary values by taking a random sample of original dataset and then sort it, and divide it to p subset.

The cost of making and sorting of sample itself is small compared to the cost of the rest of the algorithm. We consider how we can implement the sample sort on a chip-scale SIMD architecture.

Since the dataset is larger than the size of the on-chip memory. we need the following two-stage algorithm.

1. We first divide the original data of size N to subset of size n, where n is small enough that n data can fit to the on-chip memory.
2. To do so, we first read n data, and divide them to N/n subset and write back to the main memory.
3. After the above was done for all of N/n subset, we now have N/n partitioned subset. We then apply essentially the same sample sort procedure, but now for p subset where p is the number of PEs.

In the first stage, PEs should somehow divide the data to N/n subset. One possibility would be first distribute the data to all p PEs, let all of them sort data, and then conditionally output and write back the data. This is what was called "vector compression", as shown in Listing 5.6

Listing 5.6 Examole of vector compression

```
int ic=0;
for (int i=0; i< n; j++){
  if (some condition) b[ic++]= a[i];
}
```

What we need is to apply this kind of compression while transferring the data from the on-chip memory to the off-chip memory. This operation is relatively simple to implement in hardware. Note that when we transfer the data from off-chip memory to on-chip memory, we do not need any transform.

In the second stage, we want to perform the sample sort, but now for the data of size n distributed to p PEs. The simplest (and a bit inefficient) approach is to use the same compressing write to the external memory again. This however increases the necessary amount of off-chip memory access. We could also implement the bitonic sort, if the on-chip network have the topology of fat tree as in the case of GRAPE-DR or MN-Core. The performance of the bitonic sorting would be determined by the total bandwidth of the top level of the fat tree, and if it is larger than that of the external memory bandwidth, bitonic sorter would outperform the sample sort using the off-chip memory. Thus, the additional cost of the on-chip network necessary to make the bitonic sort efficient enough is not very large.

5.5.2 Off-Chip DRAM Access

Here, we consider the DRAM access pattern for the temporal blocking. We need to read/write the surfaces of the region to be integrated. This is similar to the vector compression, except that we need the reverse operation, vector decompression. For the decompression to work, the pattern of communication (which PE receive which data) should be known to the network node. It can be either fixed or data-dependent. both can be implemented by adding some data selection mechanism at each level of the on-chip tree network. Thus, here again, the additional cost would be small.

From the viewpoint of the power efficiency, the most important design parameter is the DRAM bandwidth. The access cost of DRAM chips is of the order of 5–10 pJ/bit, and it would not decrease very rapidly in the future. The power consumption consists of two parts. One is the power consumption of the DRAM memory cell itself, which is of the order of 5 pJ/bit in the case of LPDDR4X memory. The other is the energy consumption of I/O, which is determined by the wire capacitance and the output swing voltage. Thus, the key for the reduction in the necessary power is to make the connection between the DRAM chip and the processor chip as short as possible, and the swing voltage as small as possible. This is the essential reason why HBM DRAMs are better than traditional DDR or GDDR DRAMs.

The power consumption of DRAM cell is difficult to reduce, since the reduction of the cell capacitance and operating voltage are reaching their limits. Thus, in order to keep improving the performance of processor chips, it is very important to reduce the relative bandwidth of DRAM. For example, if we have a processor with B/F = 4 for double precision operation, it consumes at least 160 pJ per operation, and the performance per watt cannot exceed 6.6 GF/W. With B/F = 0.1, in principle we can reach 250 GF/W, and with 0.01 2.5 TF/W. In practice, as we have already discussed, the cost of moving data within the processor chip can be higher, and thus for practical design consideration we should make the raw power consumption of the DRAM cell to be around 10% of the total power or less. Thus, if we aim at, for example, 500 GF/W for double precision operation, which is a factor of 10 higher than what is available at chip level as of early 2021, our target B/F for external memory bandwidth should be 0.005. For a 100 TF processor, the required memory bandwidth is 500 GB/s, which is high but can be achieved with the technology currently available, such as HBM2 and GDDR6. For a 10 TF processor, the required memory bandwidth is reduced to 50 GB/s, which can be achieved with cost-effective components such as LPDDR4. The B/F number of 0.005 sounds extreme, but our analysis has shown that this number is sufficient for particles, dense matrices and structured mesh calculations. Thus, apparently, we can go around the "memory wall" for the next factor of ten improvement in the power efficiency, and probably a few times more.

5.5.3   Chip-to-Chip Communications Network for Deep Learning and Unstructured-Mesh Calculations

We have seen that the necessary network B/F numbers for both deep learning and unstructured mesh calculations are around $0.001 \sim 0.002$. Not surprizingly, this value is smaller than necessary memory bandwidth. The power consumption of SERDES (Serializer/Deserializer) circuit is currently of the order of $2.5 \sim 10\,\mathrm{pJ/bit}$ [35], and thus the power consumption would be smaller than that of the external memory. Optical connection may add another $10 \sim 20\,\mathrm{pJ/bit}$. Since most of the connections can be in copper cables, we believe it is reasonable to assume that the typical energy consumption will be $10\,\mathrm{pJ/bit}$ or less.

One practical problem is what kind of network topology and network node functionalities are necessary. In the current large-scale parallel deep-learning applications, the key features are low-latency, high-bandwidth reduction and broadcast. In other words, we need a very fast implementation of an MPI function, `MPI_ALLREDUCE`. At present, some of Infiniband switches support reduction operation in the switch and achieve the throughput comparable to that of point-to-point connection [36]. Therefore, it is possible to use standard Infiniband NICs and switches. However, the price might be too high.

5.5.4   Support for FP64, FP32 and FP16 or Other Mixed-Precision Operations

This is rather obvious requirement, if the processor should support a wide range of applications, from deep learning, for which FP16 matrix-matrix multiplication is important, to structured and unstructured mesh calculations, for which FP64 operations are important.

One question would be how we design the arithmetic unit. Until recently, even when a processor supported multiple formats like FP16, 32 and 64, they did so as SIMD vector operations. For example, the peak performance of NVIDIA P100 for FP16, FP32 and FP64 are 21.2, 10.6 and 5.3 TF. In this case, the additional circuit size for FP32 operation is small compared to that for FP64, and that for FP16 is even smaller.

However, NVIDIA V100 introduced a new way to organize low-precision arithmetic units with the support for matrix-matrix multiplication in FP16. Its FP16 performance is 16 times higher than that for FP64. The circuit size of FP16 matrix-matrix multiplier unit (64 FMA operations) is not much smaller than that for four FP64 arithmetic unit. NVIDIA A100 then added the support for matrix operations in FP64 (but not in FP32).

Nothing is known about how NVIDIA actually implements the FP unit, but we can extract some information by comparing the specifications of NVIDIA A100 and NVIDIA GeForce RTX3090 (see Table 5.3). For both processors, FP32 performance

Table 5.3 NVIDIA A100
and GeForce RTX3090

	A100	RTX3090
Process	TSMC N7	Samsung 8N
# Cuda core	6912	10496
# trs	54B	28.3B
# Tensor core	432	328
# Clock (MHz)	1410	1695
FP16 (TF)	312	142
FP32 (TF)	19.5	36
FP64 (TF)	19.5	1.1
SM (MB)	17.4	10.25
L2D61 (MB)	40.0	6.0

is consistent with the assumption that one Cuda core does one FMA. One Tensor core of A100 performs 256 FMA operations per clock, while that of RTX 3090 128 FMA operations.

The fact that they can change the performance ratio of a Cuda core and a Tensor core seems to suggest that the two types of cores are actually implemented as separate units. In addition, FP64 Tensor core and FP16 Tensor core are also implemented as separate units.

In Sect. 4.8, we have seen that the transistor efficiency of NVIDIA A100 is high, but not extremely high. Thus, it is probably possible to have separate functional units for floating-point operations with different precisions. However, if we are to design a processor with much higher transistor efficiency, we cannot afford to implement separate units for different precisions, and should try a design in which large blocks such as the multipliers are shared by functional units for different precisions.

5.6   The Reference SIMD Processor

In the next two chapters, we will discuss the software perspective and try to "predict" the future. Before going into detailed discussions on software, we need a more clear image of how we program chip-scale SIMD processors. For this purpose, in this section we present a reference design of our proposed architecture and its execution model. We assume an extension of the GRAPE-DR architecture with support for 2, 4, 8-way SIMD operation for FP64, FP32 and FP16 operations, as well as matrix-vector multiplication of size 2, 4 and 8 for FP64, FP32 and FP16 operations. For FP16 matrix-vector multiplication, we assume that the result is stored in the FP32 format. These FP operations are done in matrix-vector multiplication units.

As in the case of GRAPE-DR, we assume that for all operations, we can specify conversion between FP64 and FP32 format, and this can be done without reducing the instruction throughput. The integer ALU exists as a separate unit, but shares the same register file and other memory units.

Figure 5.8 shows the block diagram of the processor element in our reference design. This architecture is very similar to that of GRAPE-DR, except that the floating point multiplier and the adder in GRAPE-DR are replaced by single matrix-vector multiplication/FMA (MatV/FMA) unit.

We assume the same microarchitecture as that of GRAPE-DR. Thus, the instructions are all vector instructions with the fixed vector length of four.

Figure 5.9 shows the chip level structure. In the lowest level, we have PEs. They form a broadcast block (BB), in which all PEs are connected to a single "broadcast memory" (BM). The content of BM can be broadcasted to all PEs under it, and various reduction operations (sum, logical and/or, max/min) can be performed for data read from all PEs. These broadcast/reduction functions were implemented on GRAPE-DR. We also add data-dependent serialize and deserialize operations. In the "serialize" operation, data are read from PEs with "active" flags, and they are stored to the consecutive locations in BB. The flags for the serialize operation are taken from the mask registers of PEs. The deserialize operation does the reversal of serialize, and here flags are taken from the special registers in the BB unit.

At the top level of the chip, we have one top-level broadcast memory (TBM). What can be done between TBM and BB is essentially the same as that between BM and PEs: broadcast/reduction and serialize/deserialize.

The off-chip DRAM and host interface communicate only with TBM. One question is if this architecture can support the sufficient memory bandwidth. Consider

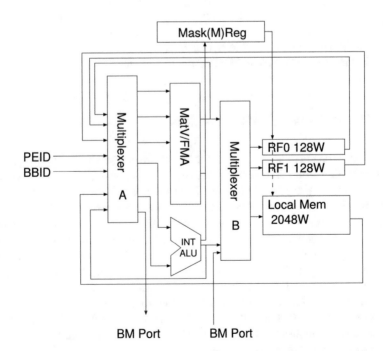

Fig. 5.8 The reference processor element

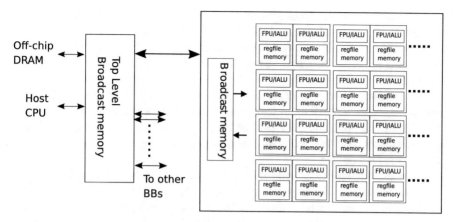

Fig. 5.9 The reference processor top levels structure

the following numbers. Each PE operates at 1 GHz clock, one BB contains 64 PEs, one chip contains 64 BBs. One PE has the double-precision peak performance of 8 Gflops, and one chip 32 Tflops. These numbers are possible with the current semiconductor technology like TSMC N7 or Samsung 8N. The minimal memory bandwidth we need is given by B/F = 0.005 and 160 GB/s. This bandwidth requires 1280 wires driven at 1 GHz clock. It does not consume too much area and the power consumption is small.

If we make the processor chip a factor of two smaller, the number of wires in the top-level tree also becomes a factor of two smaller. In addition, the length of each wire becomes smaller by a factor close to $1/\sqrt{2}$. Thus, both the area and power consumption of the top-level tree is reduced by a factor $2\sqrt{2}$, while the power consumption of PEs is reduced by a factor of two. Thus, it is generally better to make the chip size small, as far as it is large enough to run applications efficiently.

In any case, we conclude that with B/F = 0.005, a simple structure shown in Fig. 5.9 does not require too much chip area or power consumption.

If we want a higher B/F number, say 0.1, the design of the top-level structure becomes a much more difficult problem. One option is to make multiple groups of BBs and connect DRAM chips directly to these groups.

In the rest of this section, we give details of PE, BM and TBM.

5.6.1 PE

One PE has two functional units (MatV/FMA and IALU), three memory units (RF0, RF1 and LM), multiplexers to connect them, and control logics. We discuss each of them here.

The MatV/FMA unit takes up to three input operands and generates one output. Integer ALU (IALU, denoted as INT ALU in Fig. 5.8) takes two input operands and generates one output. In addition to these functional units, there are one port to send data to the broadcast memory, and one port to accept the data from the broadcast memory.

For the matrix-vector multiplication, we assume that we store the matrix to the internal registers of MatV units, and we have two set of the registers. Thus, for FP16, FP32 and FP64 operations, we need sixteen, eight and four 128-bit registers. Thus, we have matrix load (mload) instruction and matrix-vector multiplication-and-add (mmuladd) instruction.

There are three memory units in each PE: a local memory (LM) and two register files (RF0 and RF1). LM is a usual SRAM unit with one read/write port of the width of 256 bits. Its address is offset in the unit of 64-bit word from the base address register (BAR at logically address 128 of RF0). The offset is ether the content of the address prefix register (APR, also logically addresses 132 to 136 of RF0), or an immediate value with a given stride for vector operation. The read/write operations in 128-bit width can be unaligned, while 256-bit read/write must be aligned to 256-bit word. RFx is a dual-port SRAM unit with the word width of 256 bits. All ports can be accessed as 128-bit ports. The address change to the register files in vector operations is the constant addition with given stride (can be zero, broadcast of single word is also possible).

This memory structure might look odd. A conventional processor design would have load-store architecture, where the memory and functional units can communicate only through the register file. As we discussed this architecture was introduced with CDC 6600, in which the cycle time of the main memory has become the bottleneck. With a relatively small on-chip memory in our reference design, the latency and cycle time of LM is the same as that of RFx. In addition, the power consumption of read/write operations to SRAM units depends only weakly to the depth (the number of words) of them. Therefore, there is no logical reason to store the content of LM to RFx before it is fed to functional units. By bypassing RFx, we can minimize the number of read/write operations for RFx.

Compared with the memory architecture of GRAPE-DR, there are two differences. One is that the two-read-one-write (2R1W) register file of GRAPE-DR is replaced by two one-read-one-write register files. This is simply because the multi-read register files are not available as the standard IP. We can of course implement a 2R1W register file by writing the same data to two 1R1R register files, but then there is no reason to make it possible to write different data to the two register files.

Another difference is that we have removed the T-register, a four-word working register which can store the result of one instruction. In GRAPE-DR, it is also used as the direct feedback path, which provide the result of the current instruction to the next instruction. We found most of the use of the T-register is this direct feedback. Therefore we remove the T-register and added the explicit direct feedback path from arithmetic units to the input multiplexer.

There are also vector mask registers (MReg). Its contents can be set from flags from MatV/FMA or IALU. the content of Mreg can be used to control the write operations to all of LM and RFx.

Finally, there is one I/O port to the broadcast memory. It has the width of 256 bits.

Since this is a chip-scale SIMD processor, there is no reason to limit one instruction word to 32 or 64-bit length. This means there is no need for the superscalar operation, since we can make the instruction word long enough to specify the operation of all units in each instruction word. Thus, an "instruction word" for this reference design actually specifies the operation of each unit in a PE during the vector operation. In that sense, the instruction for our reference processor is very close to the horizontal microcode, except that it is a vector instruction and that the data flow for one operation, going through the pipeline structure, is specified. For example, for MatV/FMA unit with three input ports (ports A, B and C), the instruction word specifies which of the seven input of multiplexer A is fed to each port. The same is true for all input ports of all units. For the actual operation of MatV/FMA, we need to specify the word length, the operation mode (matrix or vector FMA, FMUL or FADD). In the vector FMA mode, $\pm A * B \pm C$ is calculated. Thus signs should be specified. In the matrix mode, the operation is $\pm M * B \pm C$, where M is the matrix stored in the matrix register. Thus, port A can use used to store the other window of the matrix register, and its address should be given.

It is desirable to have some way to transpose matrices, and a straightforward way is to add the mode to load matrix registers the transposed matrix.

For IALU, opcode and word length should be given. We can add some of important operations for specific applications, such as the initial guess for the inverse square root, rectified linear unit, and ceiling to IALU. Their gate counts are small and they can improve the overall performance of applications significantly.

The PEID and BBID inputs to multiplexer A give the identity of PE. Location-dependent operations can be done using these IDs. They are supplied only to port A of IALU.

For memory units, what need to be specified are the input of multiplexer B, address, word width, and the address mode (for LM, use of APR), and address inclement for vector operation.

Since one instruction word actually specifies the operations of all functional units, what can be expressed in one word is limited to what is actually possible in hardware. For example, if the MatV/FMA unit is in FMA mode and takes the outputs of all of RF0, RF1 and LM, IALU cannot specify inputs from these units, unless it happens to need the data from the same address. Also, because of the access latency of the SRAM units, the result of one instruction written to RFx is not available to the next instruction. It is available to the instruction after the next one. In order to relax these limitations, the outputs of MatV/FMA and IALU are directly fed to multiplexer A, so that they are available as the operand to the next instruction. Thus, in assembly language, we can write something like Listing 5.7.

Listing 5.7 Example of assembly language for the reference architecture

```
dpfabs $ra0v1
dpfma  $10v1   $ialufb   $rb0v1   $rb0v1 ; fabs $ra4v1
dpfma  $14v1   $ialufb   $rb4v1   $rb041 ; fabs $ra8v1
```

In this example, dpabs is the double-precision floating-point absolute value, executed in IALU, and dpfma is the double-precision FMA operation. In the first line, addresses 0–3 of RF0 is read and the absolute value is calculated in IALU. The result of this instruction is not written to anywhere, but is available as the feedback operand to the next instruction as $ialufb. In the next line, FMA operation is done for local memory with addresses 0–3, the feedback from IALU, and address 0–3 of RF1. The result is then stored to address 0–3 of RF1. At the same time, fabs operation for address 4–7 of RF0 is performed in IALU.

5.6.2   BM

Here we describe the data transfer operation between BM and PEs. The possible transfer types are

1. broadcast from BB to PEs (bm bcast)
2. reduction from PEs to BB (bm dfsum etc.)
3. deserialization (distribute data from BM to PEs (bm distribute)
4. serialization (gather data from PEs to BM (bm gather)
5. copy mask register data from PEs to BM for serialization (bm getmask).

We assume bm getmask can be issued at the same instruction cycle as other BM instructions. Only one of two downward (bcast or distribute) instructions can be issued at one time. The same is true for upward instructions (dfsum etc. and gather). The serialize/deserialize instructions take multiple, but fixed, instruction cycles, and while the upward path is busy with gather, neither gather or dfsum etc. can be issued. This means the assembler software should detect this. The hardware has no interlocking function. The same is true for distribute and bcast. The serialize operation reads one 128-bit word from the local memory of each PE and write them to the consecutive location of BM, using the mask register to compress the read vector. The deserialize operation do the reverse operation of serialize. A simple design would take 64 clock cycles, and thus 16 instruction steps, to finish one serialize/deserialize operation. We could make this part somewhat faster without increasing the total hardware too much.

The bcast operation takes one BM memory address and one PE memory address. The transfer width is fixed to 128 bits. The reduction operation has a large number of variations due to the data type (FP64, FP32 and FP16, denoted by d, s and h) and operations. The list of possible operations is given in Table 5.4

Since the reduction logic need to take reduction of a large number of data, the number of pipeline stages would be larger than that for MatV/FMA. Therefore,

Table 5.4 The reduction operations

Name	Description
(h/s/d)fsum	Floating point reduction
(h/s/d)max	Float/int maximum
(h/s/d)min	Float/int minimum
(h/s/d)isum	Integer reduction
Band	Bitwise and
bor	Bitwise or
(h/s/d)land	Logical and
(h/s/d)lor	Logical or

we assume that for BM operations, the results of one instruction are available to instruction three cycles later (cycle $i + 3$ for instruction at cycle i). Since each instruction cycle contain four clock periods, this means we allow the latency of 12 clock cycles.

The syntax for the data transfer between BM and PE would be

bm *operation source destination* [*maskid*]

Here, *operation* is bcast, dist, gat, or one of the operations listed in Table 5.4, *source* and *destination* are the start addresses of either one of storage elements of PE or BM, and *maskid* is the index of the mask register.

5.6.3 TBM

The data transfer between TBM and BM is essentially the same as that for BM and PE, except

- the data transfer width is 32 FP64 words (2048 bits).
- The "mask register" now indicate the number of word actually transferred from/to PEs.

Since the data need to travel a large distance from TBM to BBs, the necessary number of pipeline stages is very large. Since we assume relatively low clock frequency, 32 clock cycles would be reasonable to travel a distance of the order of the chip size. Therefore we assume that the results of the TBM-BM transfer instruction issued at instruction cycle i is available to instructions $i + 8$ and later.

The syntax for the data transfer between TBM and BM is

tbm *operation source destination* [*maskid*]

We can see that the instruction format is the same as that for the transfer between BM and PE.

5.6.4 DRAM Interface

We only allow block transfer between DRAM and TBM. One problem with DRAM is that its response time is not fixed because of the automatic refresh cycles. Thus, we need to introduce some waiting mechanism for TBM-BM transfer (and thus also for BM and PE instructions, because they are locked to TBM-BM instruction). Each DRAM-TBM transfer command is associated with a tag, for which one instruction can wait for the completion. We allow the DRAM read command pre-issued, in the sense that the actual write to TBM can wait until the instruction execution reached the specified point. In this way we can hide the DRAM access latency fairly well.

5.6.5 Host Data Interface

Host data interface is again essentially the same as the DRAM interface, except that the data transfer operation can be issued from the host. For the device-issued data transfer, the host memory address should be specified in the separate address registers which is writable from the host by programmed I/O (PIO) write operations. If the host initiates the data transfer, it is important that it can do so with a minimal number of PIO writes, ideally one, since the PIO write throughput of modern processors can be very low.

5.6.6 Instruction Fetch/Issue

Finally, we should describe how the instruction words are fetched and issued. In the case of GRAPE-DR, the actual chip design itself did not address this issue, since the instruction is fed from an external FPGA chip, on which we implemented the instruction memory and the sequencer logic to issue instructions. The idea for the reference design is similar. The logic to generate the instruction stream is not in the reference design. For a large number of applications, it is sufficient to supply the instruction stream generated without looking at the calculation result of PEs. In some cases, however, data-dependent generation of the instruction stream is necessary. One example is the swapping of two rows which appears in the HPL benchmark (solving dense linear system). Consider the case we have reached row (and column) i of the input matrix A of size n in the usual Gauss elimination procedure or LU factorization. For the remaining part of the matrix, we first find the max value of a_{pi} for $i \leq p \leq n$ and its location p, and swap a_{pk} and a_{ik} ($i \leq k \leq n$).

The matrix A is either in the local memories of PEs or the external DRAM. In either case, the instruction to be generated depends on the actual value of p. Thus, there should be some way for the instruction generation logic to access the results of operations. This can be implemented by making a shadow copy of a small area of TBM readable from the instruction generation logic. In the actual chip design, the instruction generation logic can be external FPGA chip or embedded FPGA IP.

References

1. J. Makino, M. Taiji, T. Ebisuzaki, D. Sugimoto, in *Proceedings Supercomputing '94* (IEEE, Los Alamitos, 1994), pp. 429–438
2. J. Makino, T. Fukushige, M. Koga, K. Namura, Publ. Astron. Soc. Japan **55**, 1163 (2003)
3. J. Makino, K. Hiraki, M. Inaba, in *Proceedings of SC07* (ACM, New York, 2007), pp. (Online)
4. J. Makino, H. Daisaka, T. Fukushige, Y. Sugawara, M. Inaba, K. Hiraki, Procedia Comput. Sci. **4**, 888 (2011). Proceedings of the International Conference on Computational Science, {ICCS} 2011. https://doi.org/10.1016/j.procs.2011.04.094. https://www.sciencedirect.com/science/article/pii/S1877050911001529
5. J. Makino, M. Taiji, *Special Purpose Computers for Scientific Simulations – The GRAPE systems* (John Wiley and Sons, Chichester, 1998)
6. A.W. Appel, SIAM J. Sci. Stat. Comput. **6**, 85 (1985)
7. J. Barnes, P. Hut, Nature **324**, 446 (1986)
8. L. Greengard, V. Rokhlin, J. Comput. Phys. **73**, 325 (1987)
9. L. Greengard, V. Rokhlin, in *Vortex Methods*, ed. by C. Anderson, C. Greengard, Lecture Notes in Mathematics, no. 1360 (Springer-Verlag, Berlin, 1988), pp. 121–141
10. D. Sugimoto, Y. Chikada, J. Makino, T. Ito, T. Ebisuzaki, M. Umemura, Nature **345**, 33 (1990)
11. J. Makino, T. Ito, T. Ebisuzaki, Publ. Astron. Soc. Japan **42**, 717 (1990)
12. T. Ito, T. Ebisuzaki, J. Makino, D. Sugimoto, Publ. Astron. Soc. Japan **43**, 547 (1991)
13. S.K. Okumura, J. Makino, T. Ebisuzaki, T. Fukushige, T. Ito, D. Sugimoto, E. Hashimoto, K. Tomida, N. Miyakawa, Publ. Astron. Soc. Japan **45**, 329 (1993)
14. J. Makino, Astrophys. J. **369**, 200 (1991)
15. J. Makino, S.J. Aarseth, Publ. Astron. Soc. Japan **44**, 141 (1992)
16. D.E. Shaw, M.M. Deneroff, J.S.K. Ron O. Dror, R.H. Larson, C.Y. John K. Salmon, B. Batson, K.J. Bowers, M.P.E. Jack, C. Chao, J. Gagliardo, C.R.H. J.P. Grossman, D.J. Ierardi, J.L.K. István Kolossváry, T. Layman, M.A.M. Christine McLeavey, R. Mueller, Y.S. Edward, C. Priest, J. Spengler, B.T. Michael Theobald, S.C. Wang, in *Proceedings of the 34th Annual International Symposium on Computer Architecture (ISCA '07)* (ACM, 2007), pp. 1–12
17. I. Ohmura, G. Morimoto, Y. Ohno, A. Hasegawa, M. Taiji, Philos. Trans. R. Soc. A Math. Phys. Eng. Sci. **372**(2021), 20130387 (2014). https://doi.org/10.1098/rsta.2013.0387. https://royalsocietypublishing.org/doi/abs/10.1098/rsta.2013.0387
18. A. Rodchenko, A. Nisbet, A. Pop, M. Luján, in *Euro-Par 2015: Parallel Processing. Euro-Par 2015*. Lecture Notes in Computer Science, vol. 9233 (Springer, Berlin, Heidelberg, 2015)
19. J. Makino, M. Taiji, T. Ebisuzaki, D. Sugimoto, Astrophys. J. **480**, 432 (1997)
20. J. Makino, Publ. Astron. Soc. Japan **43**, 621 (1991)
21. N. Nakasato, J. Makino, in *2009 IEEE International Conference on Cluster Computing and Workshops (CLUSTER)* (IEEE Computer Society, Los Alamitos, 2009), pp. 1–9. https://doi.org/10.1109/CLUSTR.2009.5289127. https://doi.ieeecomputersociety.org/10.1109/CLUSTR.2009.5289127
22. KFCR Corp. Goose: Domain-specific compiler (2009). http://www.kfcr.jp/goose-e.html
23. S. Motoki, H. Daisaka, N. Nakasato, T. Ishikawa, F. Yuasa, T. Fukushige, A. Kawai, J. Makino, J. Phys. Conf. Ser. **608**, 012011 (2015). https://doi.org/10.1088/1742-6596/608/1/012011
24. H. Daisaka, N. Nakasato, T. Ishikawa, F. Yuasa, K. Nitadori, J. Phys. Conf. Ser. **1085**, 052004 (2018). https://doi.org/10.1088/1742-6596/1085/5/052004
25. M. Iwasawa, D. Namekata, K. Nitadori, K. Nomura, L. Wang, M. Tsubouchi, J. Makino, Publ. Astron. Soc. Japan **72**(1) (2020). https://doi.org/10.1093/pasj/psz133
26. S. Oshino, Y. Funato, J. Makino, Publ. Astron. Soc. Japan **63**, 881 (2011)

27. G.E. Blelloch, C.E. Leiserson, B.M. Maggs, C.G. Plaxton, S.J. Smith, M. Zagha, in *Proceedings Symposium on Parallel Algorithms and Architectures* (Hilton Head, SC, 1991), pp. 3–16
28. D. Parkinson, J. Litt, *Massively Parallel Computing with the DAP* (Pitman Publishing, London, 1990)
29. K.E. Batcher, in *AFIPS '68 (Spring): Proceedings of the April 30–May 2, 1968, Spring Joint Computer Conference* (ACM, New York, 1968), pp. 307–314
30. J. Makino, P. Hut, Comput. Phys. Rep. **9**, 199 (1989)
31. J. Makino, J. Comput. Phys. **87**, 148 (1990)
32. M. Wolfe, in *Proceedings Supercomputing '89* (IEEE, Los Alamitos, 1989), pp. 655–664
33. J. Ragan-Kelley, C. Barnes, A. Adams, S. Paris, F. Durand, S. Amarasinghe, ACM SIGPLAN Not. **48**(6), 519 (2013)
34. T. Muranushi, J. Makino, Procedia Comput. Sci. **51**, 1303 (2015)
35. H. Hwang, J. Kim, Electronics **9**(7) (2020). https://doi.org/10.3390/electronics9071113. https://www.mdpi.com/2079-9292/9/7/1113
36. R.L. Graham, L. Levi, D. Burredy, G. Bloch, G. Shainer, D. Cho, G. Elias, D. Klein, J. Ladd, O. Maor, A. Marelli, V. Petrov, E. Romlet, Y. Qin, I. Zemah, in *High Performance Computing. ISC High Performance 2020*. Lecture Notes in Computer Science, vol. 12151 (Springer, Cham, 2020). https://doi.org/10.1007/978-3-030-50743-5_3

Chapter 6
Software

6.1 Traditional Approaches

Right now, the important standards for the programming of accelerators are OpenCL [1], OpenACC [2] and OpenMP [3]. The most widely used is of course Cuda. The basic ideas behind Cuda and OpenCL are rather similar. So let us start with OpenCL.

Fig. 6.1 The memory model of the OpenCL framework

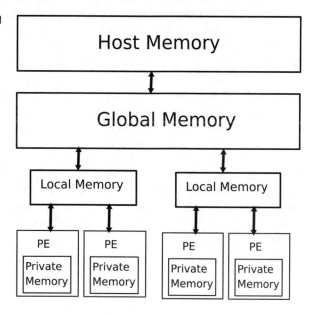

Figure 6.1 presents the memory model of OpenCL. The structure itself is actually very similar to the structure of our reference design in Fig. 5.9. However, the implied programming models are quite different. The OpenCL model is designed with GPGPUs from NVIDIA and AMD in mind. They have large and reasonably fast external memory and one or two levels of cache and/or local memories. The global memory is the largest, and then local memories, and the private memories of PEs are the smallest.

In our reference design, we have a similar hierarchy of TBM, BM and local memory (here, our local memory is local to PEs and thus corresponds to the private memory in OpenCL). The total size of local memories is much larger than that of BM or TBM. Of course, the off-chip DRAM is larger, but it is not connected directly to the host memory.

Another, more important difference is that in OpenCL PEs can directly access the variables in the global memory through __global pointers. Thus, the addition of two matrices in the global memory in OpenCL can be expressed as Listing 6.1.

Listing 6.1   Example of vector addition in OpenCL

```
__kernel void MatrixAdd(__global double* pA,
                        __global double* pB,
                        __global double* pC)
{
  const int id = get_global_id(0);
  pC[id] = pA[id] + pB[id];
}
```

In our reference design, assuming that the data are in TBM, we first need to move the data to BM, and then PE, and then add the elements, and send the results back to BM and then TBM. All of these five operations can be overlapped, and should be expressed as overlapped operations at the assembly language level to be actually overlapped. A more subtle difference in the semantics is that in OpenCL it is assumed that PEs can access the global memory through their own pointers. In our reference design, we removed this capability from PEs and only allow broadcast/reduction and serialize/deserialize operations. They are sufficient to actually implement the applications, but they cannot be expressed with the current syntax of OpenCL. We could have something like Listing 6.2. In this example, keywords __bm and __local mean that the variables are in BM or LM. The parametric types TBB and BTB mean they are operands for serialize/deserialize operations between TBM and BM, and TBB is on the TB side and BTB is on the BM side. Similarly, BLM denotes that it is the BM-side operand for serialize/deserialize operation. The double2 type is the 128-bit word with two double-precision floating-point numbers.

Listing 6.2 Example of array addition for the reference design

```
__kernel void MatrixAdd(__global double* pA,
                        __global double* pB,
                        __global double* pC)
{
    __bm double bmA[BUFFSIZE];
    __bm double bmB[BUFFSIZE];
    __bm double bmC[BUFFSIZE];
    __local double2 la;
    __local double2 lb;
    for (int i=0; i<4;i++){
        bmA[i*32] = *((TBB<double> *) pA+i*2048);
        bmB[i*32] = *((TBB<double> *) pB+i*2048);
    }
    la = *((BLM<double>*)bmA);
    lb = *((BLM<double>*)bmB);
    *((BLM<double>*)bmB) = la+lb;
    for (int i=0; i<4;i++){
        *((TBB<double>*) pC+i*2048) = bmC[i*32];
    }
}
```

Compared to the OpenCL example of Listings 6.1 and 6.2 looks more complex.
However, we can simplify this example by introducing the types associated with the
direct serialize/deserialize operations between TBM and LM, which we call TBLM.
Now we have Listing 6.3. We can see that this code now looks simpler than the
OpenCL example. The difference actually reflects the conceptual difference in the
design of the memory hierarchy. In OpenCL, each PE accesses the global memory
using its pointer. Thus, each PE need to generate its address to access from its id. On
the other hand, in our example, the block of data in TBM is distributed by hardware
to BMs and then PEs. Thus, PEs do not need to generate their addresses to access
TBM.

Listing 6.3 Example of array addition for the reference design with support for direct copy
operations between TBM and LM

```
__kernel void MatrixAdd(__global double* pA,
                        __global double* pB,
                        __global double* pC)
{
    __local double2 la;
    __local double2 lb;
    la = *((TBLM<double>*)pA);
    lb = *((TBLM<double>*)pB);
    *((TBLM<double>*)pC) = la+lb;
}
```

Thus, though it might make sense to use the syntax similar to that used in
OpenCL to express the computing kernels (operations on the variables in the local
memory), we need a different way to express the data transfer operations between
different levels of the memory hierarchy. We could introduce the data types and
extended assignment operators which express the serialize/deserialize operations.
For broadcast operation, we can just use usual assignments. For reduction, we

can use operators such as +=, as was used in C* language [4] for the Connection Machine.

Note that this OpenCL-like language with extended assignment expressions for serialize gives us practically complete control of the reference processor, and we can express all of algorithms we have discussed in Sect. 5.3. However, it is still a rather low level language and to let application programmers write their programs in this level is not ideal. In the next section, we discuss how the applications should be written and how they should be converted to the machine code.

6.2   How Do We Want to Describe Applications?

So far, we have discussed how we design a transistor- and power-efficient processor architecture on which we can run applications in several different categories. However, our proposed architecture is quite different from conventional processor architecture, and thus the application software developed for conventional processors would not run on the proposed architecture. Moreover, the proposed architecture requires the programming method quite different from what we have for traditional multicore systems.

Let us first discuss what is necessary to describe an application. In the following, we discuss the four categories we introduced in Chap. 3.

6.2.1   Structured Mesh

Calculations with structured mesh usually deal with the discretization of partial differential equations with boundary conditions. We decided to consider only explicit methods. Thus, the problem to be solved is specified completely by:

- the spatial difference scheme
- the time integration scheme
- the boundary condition

In many applications, the generalized coordinate system is used to represent the problem. For example, in climate modeling, we need to express the surface of a sphere in some way, and we should also express the earth surface (such as mountains). Thus, the coefficients of the difference scheme can depend on the location. However, essentially what we should specify is the above.

The spatial difference scheme can be expressed as a function which takes the values of variables at the current and its neighboring grid points with given maximum displacement. This of course can be written in a style similar to usual programming languages, assuming that we have some special operator to access the values of variables in the neighboring grid points.

The time integration can be described as the operations on the variables in one grid point. The description of the boundary condition can have various possibilities but usually some operation which depends on both the physical value of the current and neighboring grid points as well as the location or index of the grid point would be sufficient.

At present, the development of efficient programs for structured mesh applications on one HPC platform can be a very complex and difficult task, since we need to design the code so that it takes advantage of many features of modern processors such as the SIMD execution units, the hierarchical cache, and the multicore architecture. As we have already seen, the limitations of the instruction sets, such as a small number of architecture registers, makes the task more difficult.

A straightforward representation of the algorithm still runs and gives the correct answer on modern machines, and minimal compiler directives (such as `omp parallel for` ... might be enough to use multiple cores, but the performance we can achieve with such a simple approach is usually very limited. At the best, the efficiency is limited by the memory bandwidth. On the vector processors of 1980s and 1990s, this actually resulted in very high efficiency, such as 30–60% of the peak. However, as the B/F number has declined from 4 of these vector processors to around 0.1 of modern multicore processors, the efficiency we can achieve with this approach also declined to around a few percents. On some architectures which keep relatively high B/F numbers such as Fujitsu A64fx and NEC SX-Aurora, the efficiency of around 10% is possible.

Our reference design removes many of the difficulties of modern processors. Because of the SIMD architecture, all available physical registers are exposed, and the processor core has the access to the entire local memory, which is the only large on-chip memory, as the operands for arithmetic operations. Thus, unlike the modern multicore processors, the code generation for our reference design is rather simple. In the architecture with hierarchical cache, the total capacity is larger for caches closer to the main memory and thus farther from the CPU core. This means that the latency is large and the bandwidth is small. In our reference design, once the data are in the local memory, the processor core can access them with the latency and bandwidth the same as that of register file.

Thus, it seems one practical way to use our reference design for structured-mesh calculations is to develop a code generation system which takes the description of the numerical schemes such as the spatial difference, the time integration scheme and the boundary condition and generates the assembly code directly from such description.

The actual code generated can be in the OpenCL-like language discussed in Sect. 6.1, but the direct generation of assembly language is also possible and could be simpler.

In the case of the structured mesh calculations, one PE need to access the data in its neighboring PEs. In the case of OpenCL, this simply means each PE should access additional area of the global memory. The access to the global memory is expensive but can be done through usual access by PE. In our reference design, moving data from one PE to the neighboring PE can be complicated, since the data need to go through BM or in some case TBM. However, we can have library function to do this and application programmer can simply call it.

The actual procedure of the data transfer between the host and the accelerator is independent of the details of the problem, as far we are dealing with the explicit time stepping on the structured mesh. It does not make sense to let application programmers to (re-)implement this part of their programs. Therefore, the programming environment for structured-mesh applications should be some kind of DSL (domain-specific language), with which the application programmer describe the numerical scheme. The actual code generation should be done in the side of the DSL.

Once we have a specification for such a DSL, we can use it to generate efficient codes for existing architectures. We have implemented such DSL, Formura [5, 6]. It achieved a reasonable efficiency on K computer and very good efficiency on PEZY-SC2.

There have been many research projects to develop DSL for structured-mesh applications (sometimes called as stencil computation), and the fact that there are many of them suggests that it is not easy to develop something actually useful.

In our opinion, the reason why DSL for stencil computing has not become popular is that it has been very difficult to achieve high performance for stencil computing on modern multicore processors. It was much easier on vector processors, and at that time practical DSLs for solving partial differential equations such as PDEL [7] and DEQSOL [8, 9] were possible. On vector processors with B/F=4 or around, a simple and straightforward translation from the finite-difference scheme to the actual source program was sufficient to achieve high efficiency. However, with modern microprocessors with multiple SIMD execution units, out-of-order execution and hierarchical cache memories, we simply do not know how we can make best use of these features.

The basic strategy to improve the performance of structured-mesh applications on processors with low memory bandwidth is the cache blocking and ultimately the temporal blocking as we have discussed in Sect. 3.3.2. To implement the general framework for these blocking schemes is the easiest on the processor architecture with single-level fast local memory. Once we load the necessary data from the main memory to the local memory, there will be sufficient memory bandwidth and memory capacity, and a straightforward code would give good performance as in the case of vector processors. An important fact is that the performance of the code generated is predictable. The instructions to process the data in the local memory takes a predictable amount of time, since there will be no instruction stall due to pipeline bubble or cache miss. The time for data transfer between off-chip DRAM and on-chip local memory is also predictable except for the extra time due to refresh cycles.

On the other hand, how we should generate code for architectures with hierarchical cache memories is not obvious. The largest on-chip storage is usually the last-level cache, but it has large latency and limited bandwidth. Moreover, since it is a cache memory, it is difficult to control which data are loaded to which level of cache and when. Thus, an trial-and-error approach is almost always necessary to achieve a reasonable performance for structured mesh calculations on processors with conventional cache-based multicore architectures.

6.2.2 Unstructured Mesh

The difference between the structured and unstructured mesh calculations is in the connections between the grid points. In the structured mesh, grid points are organized in a multidimensional array and the neighbors can be accessed by simple address offset. In the case of the unstructured mesh, the neighbors are data dependent, but do not change during one calculation (except for adaptive remeshing and/or change in the structure). Thus, using the masked serialize/deserialize operation (with probably some more additional functionalities), we should be able to implement the data move necessary to implement unstructured mesh calculation.

6.2.3 Particles

If we use the offloading model, in which we use the reference processor only to calculate the interaction between particles, we use it essentially to emulate the GRAPE special-purpose processors. In this case, our OpenCL like language with additions to express the data transfers between TBM and BM, and BM and PE would be sufficient. To move the entire application code to PE is not very difficult, since most of application code, except for the interaction calculation. operates on the particle itself and thus closed to the local memory. For the interaction calculation, we need to implement the tree construction and the tree traversal, as we have discussed in Sect. 5.3.1. This is again best done in a DSL or a framework, which provides abstract functions or a code generation mechanism for given particle data type and interaction function. Thus, no matter whether we use the offloading model, we can use our reference processor from the FDPS framework [10], and the interaction kernel would be written in a DSL designed for that purpose, PIKG [11].

Listing 6.4 shows a minimal example of the definition of a particle class in C++. Here PIKG is the namespace for PIKG library and F64 and F64vec are names for double precision numbers and three (or two) dimensional vectors of double precision numbers. We use the softening for the gravitational interaction defined in Eq. 5.2. Thus we need to specify the value of ϵ, which is not in the particle class in Listing 6.4. In Listing 6.5, ϵ, is declared as F64 eps2. This declaration indicates that eps2 is a constant initialized at outside the interaction kernel, and an API interface to set its value is generated.

In the actual interaction body in Listing 6.5, we can see three keywords, EPI, EPJ and FORCE. These keywords specifies the definition of classes for particles which receive the forces, particles which exert the forces, and a special class which have the members to store the calculated interaction. In the simplest implementation, the class definitions for these three keywords can be the same. Thus, we can use member variables such as pos, mass, acc and pot in the description of the interaction kernel. Since PIKG has a built-in type for three-dimensional vectors, the code in Listing 6.5 is simplified compared to that in LSUMP (Listing 5.2) we discussed in Sect. 5.2.3.

Listing 6.6 shows the sample implementation of the Lennart-Jones potential used in molecular dynamics simulations. In this example conditional statements are used in several places. Thus, we can express many interaction kernels used in various simulations using PIKG.

Listing 6.4 Example of particle class for PIKG

```
#include <pikg_vector.hpp>
struct Particle{
  PIKG::F64vec pos;
  PIKG::F64vec vel;
  PIKG::F64vec acc;
  PIKG::F64    mass;
  PIKG::F64    pot;
  void clear(){
    acc = 0.0;
    pot = 0.0;
  }
};
```

Listing 6.5 PIKG example for gravitational interaction

```
F64 eps2

rij = EPI.pos - EPJ.pos
r2 = rij * rij + eps2
r_inv   = rsqrt(r2)
r2_inv = r_inv * r_inv
mr_inv  = EPJ.mass * r_inv
mr3_inv = r2_inv * mr_inv
FORCE.acc -= mr3_inv * rij
FORCE.pot -= mr_inv
```

Listing 6.6 PIKG example for Lennart-Jones potential

```
F64 l
F64 rc

dx  = EPI.rx - EPJ.rx
if dx < -0.5*l
  dx = dx + l
endif
if dx >= 0.5*l
  dx = dx - l
endif

dy = EPI.ry - EPJ.ry
if dy < -0.5*l
  dy = dy + l
```

```
endif
if dy >= 0.5*l
   dy = dy - l
endif

dz  = EPI.rz - EPJ.rz
if dz < -0.5*l
   dz = dz + l
endif
if dz >= 0.5*l
   dz = dz - l
endif

r2  = dx * dx + dy * dy + dz * dz
if r2 < rc*rc && r2 > 0.0
   r2i = 1.0 / r2
   r6i = r2i * r2i * r2i
   f = (48.0 * r6i - 24.0) * r6i * r2i
   FORCE.fx += f * dx
   FORCE.fy += f * dy
   FORCE.fz += f * dz
   FORCE.p += 4.0 * r6i*(r6i - 1.0)
endif
```

PIKG can generate the code for multiple architectures, including Intel x86 (AVX2, AVX512), Fujitsu A64fx (ARM SVE), and NVIDIA GPGPUs (Cuda), and it is straightforward to support architectures like MN-Core and our reference processor. As already discussed in Sect. 5.3.1, we could move tree construction and tree traversal functions to the accelerator, and that can be done within the FDPS framework without touching the user code. Thus, at least for particle-based simulations, by using frameworks like FDPS and automatic code generation for interaction kernels, we can write the application code which runs efficiently on multiple architectures without the need of the architecture-dependent tuning.

In practice, we should still optimize the codes within FDPS for the tree construction and the tree traversal, as well as the inter-process communication. The optimization of communication is important for HPC platforms with very large number of computing nodes such as Supercomputer Fugaku [12].

6.2.4   Dense Matrices

From the point of view of how the applications are written, the field of deep learning is quite different from other field of high-performance computing. Almost all applications are written using frameworks such as TensorFlow/Keras [13] or PyTorch [14]. There are several other frameworks like Caffe [15] and Chainer [16]. As of 2021, TensorFlow/Keras and PyTorch are most widely used. In addition, there is a standard format to represent machine learning models called ONNX [17].

Thus, for deep learning applications, there is essentially no need to support user-written codes. It is sufficient to implement the functions necessary to implement these frameworks. In addition, the functionalities required by these frameworks are similar and limited, such as the convolution and application of simple functions such as ReLU. Thus, it is relatively easy to provide support for these frameworks. Of course, this is one of the reasons why there have been a number of development projects for processors specialized for deep learning.

6.3   Summary

In this chapter, we discussed the question of how we program a chip-scale SIMD processors for actual HPC applications. The description of the computing kernel itself can be done with a framework similar to OpenCL (or Cuda), since these frameworks are designed for an SIMD execution model. The memory model is also similar, since a hierarchy of global, local and private memories of OpenCL roughly matches with TBM, BM and LM of our reference design. However, the operations supported on TBM and BM are quite different from what is assumed in OpenCL, and thus we need to add extra syntax to express the operations like broadcast/reduction and serialize/deserialize. These additions can be done using the C* language [4] for the Connection Machine.as a model. Thus, it is certainly possible to write applications, or at least the part of the applications to be offloaded to the accelerators, using this OpenCL-like framework.

In practice, however, we believe it is more practical to provide several DSLs or frameworks for important application areas. We discussed structured mesh, particles and deep learning in some detail. For structured mesh applications, there were such DSLs for vector processors, but the automatic generation of efficient codes for modern microprocessors turned out to be very difficult. It is much simpler for chip-scale SIMD processors with large local memories, and thus will be practical. We have achieved a reasonable performance with our DSL on PEZY-SC2 [6]. For particle-based simulations, we already have developed such a framework, FDPS [10]. In the field of deep learning, practically all applications are written using frameworks such as TensorFlow/Keras or PyTorch. Thus, the use of framework is already a usual practice in this field. We believe frameworks will be popular in other fields of HPC in near future.

References

1. Khronos® OpenCL Working Group. The OpenCL™ Specification. https://www.khronos.org/registry/OpenCL/specs/3.0-unified/html/OpenCL_API.html (2020)
2. OpenACC-Standard.org. The openacc® application programming interface. https://www.openacc.org/sites/default/files/inline-images/Specification/OpenACC-3.1-final.pdf (2020)
3. OpenMP Architecture Review Board. OpenMP Application Programming Interface. https://www.openmp.org/wp-content/uploads/OpenMP-API-Specification-5-1.pdf (2020)
4. J.R. Rose, J. Guy L. Steele, in *Proceedings of the Second International Conference on Supercomputing, vol. II* (1987), pp. 2–16

5. T. Muranushi, H. Hotta, J. Makino, S. Nishizawa, H. Tomita, K. Nitadori, M. Iwasawa, N. Hosono, Y. Maruyama, H. Inoue, H. Yashiro, Y. Nakamura, in *SC '16: Proceedings of the International Conference for High Performance Computing, Networking, Storage and Analysis* (2016), pp. 23–33. https://doi.org/10.1109/SC.2016.2

6. H. Tanaka, Y. Ishihara, R. Sakamoto, T. Nakamura, Y. Kimura, K. Nitadori, M. Tsubouchi, J. Makino, in *2018 IEEE/ACM 4th International Workshop on Extreme Scale Programming Models and Middleware (ESPM2)* (2018), pp. 29–36

7. A.F. Cardenas, W.J. Karplus, Commun. ACM **13**(3), 184–191 (1970). https://doi.org/10.1145/362052.362059

8. Y. Umetani, Proc. IFIP TC2/WG22, 1985 **5**, 147 (1985). https://ci.nii.ac.jp/naid/10015772035/

9. C. Konno, Y. Umetani, M. Igai, T. Ohta, Math. Comput. Simul. **31**(4), 353 (1989). https://doi.org/10.1016/0378-4754(89)90130-4. https://www.sciencedirect.com/science/article/pii/0378475489901304. Special Double Issue

10. M. Iwasawa, A. Tanikawa, N. Hosono, K. Nitadori, T. Muranushi, J. Makino, Publ. Astron. Soc. Japan **68**, 54 (2016). https://doi.org/10.1093/pasj/psw053

11. K. Nomura, Pikg (2020). https://github.com/FDPS/PIKG

12. T. Shimizu, in *2020 IEEE Asian Solid-State Circuits Conference (A-SSCC)* (2020), pp. 1–4. https://doi.org/10.1109/A-SSCC48613.2020.9336127

13. M. Abadi, P. Barham, J. Chen, Z. Chen, A. Davis, J. Dean, M. Devin, S. Ghemawat, G. Irving, M. Isard, M. Kudlur, J. Levenberg, R. Monga, S. Moore, D.G. Murray, B. Steiner, P. Tucker, V. Vasudevan, P. Warden, M. Wicke, Y. Yu, X. Zheng, in *12th USENIX Symposium on Operating Systems Design and Implementation (OSDI 16)* (USENIX Association, Savannah, GA, 2016), pp. 265–283. https://www.usenix.org/conference/osdi16/technical-sessions/presentation/abadi

14. A. Paszke, S. Gross, F. Massa, A. Lerer, J. Bradbury, G. Chanan, T. Killeen, Z. Lin, N. Gimelshein, L. Antiga, A. Desmaison, A. Köpf, E. Yang, Z. DeVito, M. Raison, A. Tejani, S. Chilamkurthy, B. Steiner, L. Fang, J. Bai, S. Chintala, Pytorch: An imperative style, high-performance deep learning library, preprint, arXiv:1912.01703 (2019)

15. Y. Jia, E. Shelhamer, J. Donahue, S. Karayev, J. Long, R. Girshick, S. Guadarrama, T. Darrell, in *Proceedings of the 22nd ACM International Conference on Multimedia* (Association for Computing Machinery, New York, 2014), MM '14, pp. 675–678. https://doi.org/10.1145/2647868.2654889

16. S. Tokui, K. Oono, S. Hido, J. Clayton, in *Proceedings of Workshop on Machine Learning Systems (LearningSys) in The Twenty-ninth Annual Conference on Neural Information Processing Systems (NIPS)* (2015). http://learningsys.org/papers/LearningSys_2015_paper_33.pdf

17. J. Bai, F. Lu, K. Zhang, et al. Onnx: Open neural network exchange. https://github.com/onnx/onnx (2019)

Chapter 7
Present, Past and Future

The future cannot be predicted, but futures can be invented.

— Dennis Gabor

7.1 Principles of High-Performance Processor Design

The purpose of this book is to provide the scientific basis, or the principles, of the design of processors for compute-intensive applications. In this section, we first present the principles which we reached. Actually, what we propose is the following single principle:

- **The principle of the high-performance processor design:** The power consumption of a processor architecture for a given application and given semiconductor technology cannot be smaller than the electric power used in the combinatorial logic of the arithmetic units with required accuracy for each operation made using the same semiconductor technology and driven by the same supply voltage.

Once we accept this principle, we can define the efficiency of a processor architecture as follows:

- **The definition of the efficiency of a processor for an application:** The power and transistor efficiencies of a processor for an application is defined as the ratio of the above minimum energy and actual energy, and also the ratio of the number of transistors used in the combinatorial logic of the arithmetic units with required accuracy and the total number of transistors.

As we have discussed in Chap. 2, we have two models in mind. The first one is the thermodynamics of heat engines. Here, the efficiency of a heat engine to convert thermal energy to mechanical energy is limited by that of the ideal Carnot cycle. This limitation is derived directly from the first and second laws of thermodynamics, and gives us two important design principles for heat engines. The first one is that the efficiency is limited by the temperature of the heat source. Thus, for any kind of heat engine with any heat source, it is very important to make the temperature

© Springer Nature Switzerland AG 2021
J. Makino, *Principles of High-Performance Processor Design*,
https://doi.org/10.1007/978-3-030-76871-3_7

of the heat source as high as possible. No matter it is a gas or steam turbine or internal-combustion engine, and no matter the heat source is a natural gas, gasoline, coal, nuclear fission or fusion, or geothermal energy. The second one is that once the temperature is given, there is a clear limit in the conversion ratio, and thus we can measure how good a design is by the ratio between the theoretical limit and the actual efficiency.

The second one is the concept of the parasite drag of airplanes. The drag force on an airplane can be divided into three parts: induced drag, friction drag and parasite drag. As far as the wing of an airplane generates lift, the induced drag will be generated. The friction drag is determined by the total surface area of an airplane, and thus can be reduced only by reducing the total surface area. Everything else is classified as the parasite drag, which should be made as small as possible.

These are just two examples of the concept of efficiency, and we have similar concepts in almost every field of engineering. In fact, it is not an oversimplification to say that one of the goals of engineering is to find "efficient" ways to do various things we need to do. The term "efficiency" in most situations mean the energy efficiency.

Thus, it is rather surprizing that the field of computer architecture for high-performance computing seemingly lacks a similar concept of the efficiency. In the following we summarize what is the current practice and how we can establish the concept of efficiency of processor architectures.

7.2 The Current Practice

In the field of processor architecture for high-performance computing, traditionally benchmarks and real application programs have been used to "measure" how good a design is. As we have seen in Chap. 3, this is exactly the method to design exascale systems in the US, Europe and Japan. This practice makes perfect sense when we select a machine for our laboratory or our institute, but if we are designing a processor to be used after 10 years from now, whether or not it is the best strategy to use use existing programs written in traditional languages as the guide for the new design is questionable. On the other hand, that is what has been done for the last half century. We have justified our practice by arguing that the value of the existing programs associated with the existing processor architecture is so large that they should run on a new architecture without significant rewrite. we even use the term "ecosystem" to justify our practice.

The problem with this practice is that it would reach a local optimal design point, and not the global optimum, even in the best case. It is clear that we should search a wider design space to find the true optimum, but the current practice prohibits such a search of a wider design space.

The fundamental problem here is that we limit the design space not from a scientific argument but as a result of economical or social evolution. If most of us believe that the current practice is the only way to advance the field, there will not be projects which try other ways. At present, the development cost of a new processor chip is huge, and it is very difficult for an academic research project, or even a commercial company, to design and fabricate a processor chip competitive with what are offered by big companies like Intel and AMD. Until 1990s most computer companies designed their own CPUs. However, right now only a few companies design their own CPUs.

7.3 Our Past

Well, then, is there no way to realize the truly optimal design? Will we be trapped in the local optimal point of multicore design with coherent shared cache and SIMD execution unit forever? If we look back at the history of computing, we do see that the transition of architecture sometimes occurred, and another one is occuring now. As we have overviewed in Chap. 2, major and minor transitions in processor architectures can be summarized as:

1. Scalar processors

   (a) pipelined
   (b) superscalar

2. Vector processors

   (a) multiple pipelines
   (b) shared-memory multiprocessors

3. Single-chip microprocessors

   (a) pipelined
   (b) superscalar
   (c) multicore
   (d) SIMD execution unit

We now have two new processor architectures.

- GPGPUs
- Deep-Learning processors

Let us first discuss the two transitions which took place in the past. The transition from scalar processors to vector processors was, practically, the transition from CDC 7600 to Cray-1, both designed by Seymour Cray. Being designed by the same person, their performance characteristics were not wildly different. Most importantly, programs which did not use the vector instructions still ran faster on Cray-1 than on CDC 7600 because of much higher clock frequency and faster SRAM memory. Thus, this is a rather exceptional case where the transition was smooth, because typical programs could see the performance improvement without rewrite.

It should be noted that Cray-1 is not the first vector processor. TI ASC [1] and CDC STAR-100 [2], which later redesigned as Cyber 205 [3], are well-known predecessors. Neither of them were great commercial success, and the primary reason was that their scalar performance was low. Their "failures" and the success of Cray-1 left the very strong influence on the design of high-performance processors, resulting in the tendency to avoid highly parallel processors. Amdahl's famous paper [4] certainly enhanced this tendency. In this paper, Amdahl declared:

> Demonstration is made of the continued validity of the single processor approach and of the weaknesses of the multiple processor approach in terms of application to real problems and their attendant irregularities.

In our opinion, this "weaknesses of the multiple processor approach" is not really related to the nature of real problems but to the way we write programs. We hope that most of the readers of this book now agree with our opinion. However, this tendency of putting too much weight on the scalar performance prevailed in 1980s and 1990s. One example is the famous bet made between Gordon Bell and Danny Hillis in 1989, described in detail in section 6.15 of [5].

> Bell bet Hillis that in the last quarter of calendar year 1995, more sustained MFLOPS would be shipped in multiprocessors using few data streams (< 100) rather than many data streams (> 1000).

So let's see how the second transition from vector processors to single-chip microprocessors took place. By 1990, some microprocessors integrated fully-pipelined double-precision floating-point arithmetic units, and thus provided the potential to outperform vector-parallel processors. TMC CM-5 was announced in 1991. Intel Paragon XP/S, based on Intel i860 was introduced in 1992, and Cray T3D in 1993. Cray T3D was based on the DEC Alpha 21064 processor, and its successor, T3E was based on the 21164 processor. The performance of T3E was improved as faster version of 21164 processor was shipped, and T3D/E had been among the fastest machines throughout 1990s. These machines all have distributed-memory architecture. CM-5 supported CM-Fortran, from which HPF was born. Cray T3x supported CRAFT. Both systems supported distributed global arrays and data-parallel operations on them, and thus it was much easier to write programs for them compared to that for systems without support for global arrays. However, efficient implementation of global arrays requires low-latency, high-bandwidth interconnection network. CM-5 had a fat tree with 40 MB/s bandwidth for each computing node with the peak speed of 128Mflops [6]. Each link of the 3D torus network of Cray T3E had the peak speed of 600 MB/s, much higher than the memory bandwidth of the DEC Alpha 21164 processor [7].

It should be noted that, for the majority of users, the transition from vector processors to microprocessor-based systems did not imply the need of rewriting their programs to take advantage of the distributed-memory architecture. By around 1992 or so, the peak speed of a single-chip microprocessor reached 100 Mflops. At that time the peak speed of the largest supercomputer in the world was around 100 Gflops. Thus, desktop workstations with the price tag of the order of 10^4 USD gave the speed around 0.1% of supercomputers with cost 10^7 USD or more.

A big supercomputer would be used by a large number of users, and usually one user runs many calculations. Thus, when shared-memory vector parallel machines in supercomputer centers were replaced by microprocessor-based distributed-memory machines, for many users, it was better to use just one processor, and for them it made more sense to have that one processor in their institutes. Obviously, there was no reason to try to rewrite their programs. They could do what they had been doing on large supercomputers on their desktop (or deskside) workstations, and the speed of workstations was growing faster than that of supercomputers. At least, it looked so in early 1990s. Thus, the transition from vector processors to single-chip microprocessors took place effectively without the rewrite of user programs for most of users.

Throughout 1990s, the performance of x86 processors from Intel and other vendors had been approaching to that of more expensive RISC microprocessors such as Sun SPARC, HP PA-RISC, DEC Alpha or MIPS R10k. This trend made "PC clusters" viable solutions. Even so, not many users used these clusters to run parallel programs. In fact, even now, most of computations in any area of science or engineering are still done on shared-memory computers. Only a small number of programs for very large-scale calculations are written for distributed-memory machines using MPI.

Thus, we can conclude that, for most of users, the rewrite of their programs was not necessary for two historical transitions of the processor architectures.

7.4 GPGPUs and Deep Learning Processors

As we mentioned in the previous section, we now have two more types of processors in addition to cache-coherent multicore processors, namely GPGPUs and processors specialized to deep learning applications.

Whether or not these new processors will really replace the old processors as in the case of vector processors and single-chip microprocessors remains to be seen. So far, existing programs need significant rewrite to take advantage of these processors. On the other hand, deep-learning applications do not need rewrite, since the dependence on the processor architecture is hidden in the frameworks such as TensorFlow.

If we look at the Top500 list, we can see that the transition to accelerator architecture has been rather slow. In November 2010 list, there were 17 systems with accelerators. In Nov 2012, the number jumped up to 61, but after that, the increase has been slow. Figure 7.1 shows the evolution of the number of systems with accelerators in the Top 500 list from year 2010 to 2020. It seems the increase is slowing down and it is not likely that accelerators will dominate the Top 500 list in foreseeable future.

One reason that the increase of the share of GPGPUs has been slow is that the advantage in the price-performance of GPUs has not been very large. Until early 2020, NVIDIA V100 offered the peak FP64 performance of 7.8TF and its price was

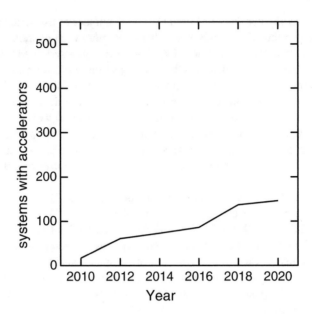

Fig. 7.1 The number of systems with accelerators in the Top 500 list

around 10K USD. On the other hand, one could buy Intel Xeon W-3175X for 3K USD. Assuming the clock speed of 2.3 GHz for fully working two AVX512 units, the peak performance of this CPU is 2.06 Tflops. Thus, there is little difference in the price performance ratios between NVIDIA V100 and Intel Xeon W-3175X. Of course, the total system price is not solely determined by the price of CPU, but that is also true for GPGPU. Thus, the difference in the price-performance ratio is rather small. A big difference is in the performance per watt, but that is not a very serious constraint in many cases. If we calculate the total cost of ownership, the system cost is still higher than the electricity cost. As we have shown in Table 4.4, the transistor efficiency of GPGPUs is not too different from that of recent CPUs. Thus, it is not surprizing that their price-performance ratios are largely similar.

Another reason is that the transition from multicore CPUs to GPGPUs still requires significant rewrite of user programs. If we want to offload a part of the calculation, it is relatively easy. Even so, we need to learn a new language and a new way to analyze and optimize our programs for each vendors of accelerators. In theory, programs written in OpenCL should run on multiple platforms, but in practice one program written in OpenCL for one hardware platform would not run efficiently on other platforms. There are other efforts to make the use of GPGPUs easier using compiler directives such as OpenACC and OpenMP (version 4.0 and later). As of early 2021, neither of them have been widely accepted. The problem is essentially the same as that of OpenCL above. We still need to rewrite the programs, and unfortunately the way the rewriting should be done depends on the hardware platform and the compiler, and is difficult to learn.

In the field of deep learning, recent GPUs gives much larger advantage over CPUs with the support of FP16 matrix-matrix multiplication. Also, GPGPUs without heavy FP64 supports (GeForce line in the case of NVIDIA) are much less expensive compared to those with FP64 support. Thus, GPGPUs first accepted in the field of deep learning because of very high price-performance ratio for FP32 matrix-matrix multiplication, and then its performance in deep learning applications was augmented with the support of FP16 matrix-matrix multiplication. For these operations, GPGPUs give the price performance ratio one order of magnitude higher than that of CPUs.

As we have stressed several times, deep learning applications are written using frameworks. Thus, once the framework supports a new processor, there is no need of rewriting the applications. The current popularity of deep learning offer a unique opportunity for new processor architectures.

In the case of the field of deep learning, there was probably several reasons why frameworks were quickly adapted. One is that the core calculation of the deep learning is fairly large matrix-matrix multiplication and thus by using vendor-optimized libraries frameworks can achieve the performance comparable to applications written for specific networks. Also, relatively simple mathematical structures of neural networks made it straightforward to implement general-purpose frameworks.

As a result of this nature of deep learning applications and frameworks for them, now one can think of designing new processors, at least for deep learning, without worrying too much about the problem of ecosystem or software assets. Once popular frameworks run on the new processor, everybody can use it "without changing their existing program".

7.5 The Future

In the previous two sections, we have analyzed the past transitions in the processor architecture and the present state. So far, major transitions took place only when a complete rewrite of programs were not required for most users. As a result, for the last three decades we have been using microprocessor-based systems. In the past three decades, microprocessors have evolved from single-core, single-issue processors to multicore, superscalar processors with SIMD execution units. The cumulative change is huge. In 1989, the Intel i860 processor had just one floating point addition unit and one floating point multiplier unit. In 2021, the Intel Skylake Xeon Platinum 8280 processor has 28 cores, each with two AVX512 SIMD units, and thus has 448 FMA units. Not all programs can make use of these 448 FMA units, but the change has been gradual, like a factor of two increase at one time, and thus has been accepted. At least there had been no other processor architecture which would run most of user programs much faster than Xeon processors without significant rewrite.

The design of Intel Skylake processor is clearly far from the theoretical optimum, with the transistor efficiency below 1%, and quite low application efficiency for many applications. Even so, if we just extrapolate from what happened in the past, it might look as if there is no chance for any new architecture to replace the present multicore processors, no matter how efficient they are. As we have already seen, the transition to GPGPUs has been slow and it seems unlikely that they will replace multicore CPUs.

The one and right now the only field where the majority of users accept new architectures such as GPGPU and other specialized processors is that of deep learning. The reason why processors with new architectures have been quickly accepted in the field of deep learning is that applications are written using frameworks and the architecture-dependent code and thus the need for the architecture-specific optimization are hidden in the framework. Only those who develop and maintain frameworks need to write architecture-specific codes.

One might argue that compilers should generate efficient codes for different architectures, and that is of course the idea behind projects like OpenACC, OpenMP (offload support of version 4.0 and later), and more recently Intel oneAPI. We certainly agree that they should, but this is not likely to happen. Right now, just to make best use of multicore processors with SIMD instruction set, we are forced to rewrite our programs. We need to change the data structure so that SIMD units can handle the data, and we need to change the loop structure to make better use of cache and multiple cores. OpenCL/OpenACC/OpenMP all have the same problem.

In Chap. 6, we discussed how we can write programs for our proposed architecture. Our conclusion is the only practical way is to develop a DSL or a framework, for each application area. We could have the programming environment not too different from OpenCL, but it seems to be a huge waste of the time of application programmers to let them write their versions of code for the data movement between the host and the processor and between the different levels of memories within the processor, since the way the data are moved is essentially determined by the application type. It should be sufficient for application programmers to provide the mathematical description of the problem, such as the finite-difference scheme for the case of structured or unstructured-mesh calculation and the functional form of the particle-particle interaction in the case of particle-based simulations. All else should be and can be done at the side of the framework.

One important advantage of frameworks is that they can generate reasonably efficient programs for existing multicore processors or GPGPUs as well, and can support distributed-memory machines by generating MPI codes. We believe the support of distributed-memory machines is extremely important, since this is what had been missing for the majority of users since the transition from vector-parallel processors to microprocessors. Writing efficient application programs using MPI is too difficult a task. At present, in addition to this already too difficult task for most of us, we have to write many lines of code so that our program can take advantage of multicore architecture, cache and SIMD execution unit. On most architecture this is an even more difficult task. We do not claim that frameworks can generate highly optimized code for any application field and any architecture, in particular because the hierarchical caches of present-day multicore processors are very difficult to use as we discussed in Sects. 2.1.5 and 5.2.3. Even so, frameworks can take advantage of multicore architectures and SIMD instruction sets reasonably well. Our FDPS framework already helped many researchers develop their own parallel programs which run on large supercomputers consisting or multicore processors.

We believe the future is in the frameworks, and they will make it possible to use processors designed to approach to the theoretical limit of efficiency. We have seen this is occuring in the field of deep learning. The question is when, not whether, will the same thing happen in other field of high performance computing.

References

1. W.J. Watson, in *Proceedings of the December 5–7, 1972, Fall Joint Computer Conference, Part I, AFIPS '72 (Fall, Part I)* (Association for Computing Machinery, New York, 1972), pp. 221–228. https://doi.org/10.1145/1479992.1480022
2. R.G. Hintz, D.P. Tate, in *Proceedings of the 6th IEEE Computer Society International Conference* (IEEE Computer Society, Washington, 1972), pp. 1–4
3. N.R. Lincoln, IEEE Trans. Comput. **C-31**(5), 349 (1982). https://doi.org/10.1109/TC.1982.1676013
4. G.M. Amdahl, in *Proceedings of the April 18–20, 1967, Spring Joint Computer Conference, AFIPS '67 (Spring)* (Association for Computing Machinery, New York, 1967), pp. 483–485. https://doi.org/10.1145/1465482.1465560
5. D.A. Patterson, J.L. Hennessy, *Computer Organization and Design, Fifth Edition: The Hardware/Software Interface*, 5th edn. (Morgan Kaufmann Publishers, San Francisco, 2013)
6. C.E. Leiserson, Z.S. Abuhamdeh, D.C. Douglas, C.R. Feynman, M.N. Ganmukhi, J.V. Hill, W. Hillis, B.C. Kuszmaul, M.A. St. Pierre, D.S. Wells, M.C. Wong-Chan, S.W. Yang, R. Zak, J. Parallel Distrib. Comput. **33**(2), 145 (1996). https://doi.org/10.1006/jpdc.1996.0033. https://www.sciencedirect.com/science/article/pii/S0743731596900337
7. S.L. Scott, et al., The Cray T3E Network: Adaptive routing in a high performance 3d torus in Proceedings of Hot Interconnects IV, pp. 147–156 (1996)

Index

© Springer Nature Switzerland AG 2021
J. Makino, *Principles of High-Performance Processor Design*,
https://doi.org/10.1007/978-3-030-76871-3

Printed in the United States
by Baker & Taylor Publisher Services